Play and leisure areas

Apart from leisure areas – such as patios basked in sunshine, courtyards closeted in privacy or elevated and sheltered decking – there are many features that especially appeal to young children. These include sandpits, swings and paddling pools, while goalposts and basketball hoops are possibilities for later years. Enriching outdoor living areas with fixed or portable barbecues creates further interest; lights and patio heaters extend their use into evening.

What are the options?

PLAY AREAS FOR CHILDREN

All play areas for young children – especially those still at the crawling and toddling stage – need to be fenced to prevent dogs defecating and urinating on the grass or sand. Swings and roundabouts need careful positioning and maintenance, while children in pools (however shallow the water) need constant supervision; also, pools should be emptied or securely covered after each use to prevent children climbing into them when not supervised.

Sand pits are simple to make yet an exciting adventure for young children.

Play areas can be a medley of slides, swings, ladders and climbing ropes.

LEISURE AREAS

Increasingly, gardens are planned to be extensions of homes – at little cost compared with commissioning an architect and builder – and a sure way to create an outdoor living area tailored to your desires. There are many ways to undertake this, including:
- **Decking:** surfaces either raised or at ground level, and formed of wood (see page 41).
- **Patios:** correctly, areas surrounded by a building that helps to create shade and tranquillity. Nowadays, any surface outdoors is considered to be a patio, and this term also includes terraces (see page 40).

Link elevated decking with a garden by using strong and attractive steps.

Multi-level patios enable slopes to be separated into several small areas.

BARBECUES AND HEATERS

'Grown-up' garden toys, such as barbecues, bottle-gas patio heaters, portable wood-burning and coal stoves, are potentially lethal unless treated with respect; toddlers and other youngsters must be kept away from them. Mains-powered lights are other dangers to health unless properly installed and annually maintained by a competent electrician; those powered by batteries or transformers are safer. Solar-powered lights are safe, and very easy to install.

KEEPING THE AREA CLEAN

Dog faeces can harbour harmful eggs and larvae of roundworms, which are particularly dangerous to children and can cause sight-threatening problems. Therefore, keep the area free from dog excreta and encourage children to wash their hands thoroughly after being in the garden and especially before handling food. Additionally, every 4–6 months worm your dog; seek advice from your local veterinary clinic. Remember that infected soil remains a danger to small children for up to six years. The faeces of cats may also be a source of infection, and are of special danger to pregnant women.

Ornamental gardens

Many garden plants are known as 'ornamentals' because of their attractive flowers or leaves. Ornamental gardens include arrangements of biennials, hardy annuals, spring- and summer-flowering bedding plants, herbaceous perennials, shrubs, trees and climbers. Some, such as hardy annuals, have a short life-span, whereas shrubs and trees will be with you for 15 years or more. Many climbers also have a long life and help to create attractive screens.

SHORT-SEASON BORDERS

- **Hardy annuals** are sown outdoors in prepared beds in spring; they flower in summer and are pulled up in early autumn and added to a compost heap. The border then needs to be dug, so that the soil's surface is exposed to winter frost, wind and rain (this helps to break down the surface soil to a fine tilth for seeds to be sown during the following spring).

Agrostemma githago 'Milas'
(Corn Cockle)

- **Spring-flowering displays** are usually formed of medleys of spring-flowering bulbs, such as tulips, and spring-flowering biennials such as wallflowers.
- **Summer-flowering displays** are formed of tender annuals that are sown in gentle warmth in greenhouses in late winter or early spring. Plants are later acclimatized (hardened off) to outdoor conditions and planted into borders when all risk of frost has passed. There are many different plants and they are inexpensive to buy in late spring or early summer.

Erysimum x allionii
(Siberian Wallflower)

Lobularia maritima
(Sweet Alyssum)

SUMMER-LONG DISPLAYS

- **Herbaceous perennials** have a durable nature, each year from late spring to early autumn creating a colourful display. Every 3–4 years plants are dug up and divided, and healthy parts from around the outside of each clump are replanted. Discard old, inner parts.

Aster sedifolius
(herbaceous Aster)

LONG-TERM FEATURES

- **Shrubs** will usually last 15 years or more; many shrubs need annual pruning to maintain a yearly display of flowers or, with a few shrubs, coloured stems, as well as to keep them healthy. Both flowering and attractively foliaged shrubs can be planted in the same border.

Cistus x dansereaui
(Rock Rose)

- **Trees** are often used as focal points in a garden, or individually in lawns. Some, such as silver birches, are ideal in small groups, perhaps surrounded by naturalized bulbs like crocuses. Most trees have a life-span of 20 years or more.

Amelanchier lamarckii
(Snowy Mespilus)

- **Mixed borders** are formed of medleys of shrubs, trees, herbaceous perennials and bulbs, with more ephemeral plants such as hardy annuals and summer-flowering bedding plants used to fill gaps, especially before the more permanent plants are fully established.

Water gardening

Garden ponds vary greatly in size and shape, being either informal or formal, and may also include waterfalls and cascades. Wildlife ponds, bog gardens and streamside areas are other possibilities. Construction methods also vary, and whereas 50 years or more ago ponds were usually formed of concrete (still a possibility, but with a different technique) there are now rigid and flexible liners, some with a short life-span and others that will last 25 years or more.

Where do I start?

WATER GARDENING OPTIONS

Concrete ponds

In earlier years, concrete ponds were usually square or rectangular, with vertical sides. This type of construction created weakness at the corners and edges. Nowadays, oval or circular ponds, with sloping sides, are better.

Raised ponds

↗ Totally or partly raised ponds are popular and help to create dominant features on patios. They can be made with flexible or rigid liners.

Mini-ponds

↗ Strong tubs create superb summer-long mini-ponds for miniature aquatic plants and a few fish, but in cold areas the tub either needs to be emptied or taken into a greenhouse or conservatory during winter. Stone sinks (above) are also popular, with an age-old look.

Using rigid pond liners

↗ Also known as moulded ponds, precast ponds and preformed ponds, they are formed of a previously shaped rigid shell that can be placed in a hole in the ground, so that its surface edges are level with the surrounding soil.

Using flexible liners

↗ Also known as pond liners, these are sheets of strong materials that are used to line holes, which later can be filled with water. They are ideal for constructing informal ponds with irregular shapes.

Mini-pools

↗ Formed of a small fountain splashing or dribbling water on large pebbles, these tiny water features are ideal for patios. They present little risk to young children, even toddlers.

Wildlife ponds

↗ With a relaxed and informal nature, they are ideal for creating havens for fish, amphibians, insects, birds and small mammals. They are full of interest.

Bog gardens

Ideal for positioning at the edge of an informal pond to create an area of moist soil in which bog-garden plants can be grown.

Producing food

What can I hope to grow?

Vegetables range from those with a short growing season, such as summer radishes, carrots and lettuces, to long-term and more permanent types like asparagus. Cabbages, cauliflowers, Brussels sprouts, potatoes and leeks also require a long growing season, but not as extensive as for asparagus, which forms a permanent bed from which spears can be cut for ten years or more. Many culinary herbs, such as parsley, can be raised from seeds.

VEGETABLES

Vegetables can be grouped in several ways. Here they are grouped by the method of raising plants.

Sown directly where plants will grow and mature; these include:
• Broad beans
• French beans
• Runner beans
• Beetroot
• Carrots
• Lettuces
• Bulbing onions
• Spring onions
• Parsnips
• Peas
• Radishes
• Spinach
• Sweetcorn
• Turnips

Initially raised in seed beds outdoors for transfer, when large enough, to their growing positions; these include:
• Asparagus (to produce 'crowns' for later planting)
• Broccoli
• Brussels sprouts
• Cabbages
• Calabrese
• Cauliflowers
• Kale
• Leeks

Sweetcorn is best sown in blocks, rather than in single rows.

Broccoli 'Red Arrow'

Cauliflower 'Dominant'

VEGETABLES (CONTINUED)

Sown in gentle warmth in greenhouses or garden frames and later planted in vegetable gardens; these include:
- Aubergines
- Celery
- Celeriac
- Early leeks
- Early onions
- Sweetcorn (can also be sown outdoors, directly in its growing position)
- Sweet peppers
- Tomatoes

Gentle warmth is essential in late winter and spring if you want to germinate seeds and raise young plants.

CULINARY HERBS

Herbs can also be grouped in several ways. Here they are grouped by the method of raising plants.

Raised from seeds; these include:
- Angelica
- Caraway
- Fennel
- Hyssop
- Parsley

Raised from cuttings; these include:
- Balm
- Rosemary
- Sage
- Thyme

Increased by division; these include:
- Balm
- Chives
- Spearmint
- Tarragon

Culinary herbs such as chives can be easily and quickly increased by dividing established clumps and replanting young pieces from around the outside.

Growing soft and tree fruits

What is the difference?

Tree fruits, such as apples and pears, are long-lived, whereas bush fruits may live perhaps only eight or so years if pruning and care are neglected. Strawberries have an even shorter life and after three years are best replaced with fresh plants. Some fruits, such as raspberries, blackberries, loganberries and other hybrid berries, are known as cane fruits. These plants are formed of long, cane-like stems that are secured to tiered wires tensioned between posts.

TREE FRUITS

Apples
Early-season varieties: picked from mid-summer to early autumn, and eaten within seven days.
Mid-season varieties: picked from early to mid-autumn, and eaten within three weeks.
Late-season varieties: picked from mid- to late autumn, and stored for up to five months, depending on the variety.

Pears
Harvesting: late summer to mid-autumn.
Eating: as soon as possible, although a few varieties last in store until early winter.

Plums
Harvesting: latter part of mid-summer to the late part of early autumn, depending on the variety.
Eating: usually, within a few days of picking.

Apricots
Harvesting: latter part of mid-summer to late summer.
Eating: within a few days of picking.

Peaches and nectarines
Harvesting: latter part of mid-summer to early autumn, depending on the variety.
Eating: fruits can be stored in a cool place for about a week.

Cherries
Harvesting: from the latter part of early summer to late summer, depending on the variety.
Eating: fruits are best eaten as soon as possible after they have been picked.

Figs
Harvesting: late summer to early autumn, depending on the variety.
Eating: fruits can be eaten immediately, or stored in a cool placed for several weeks.

Apple

Peach

SOFT FRUITS

Strawberries
Harvesting: middle part of early summer to late autumn, depending on the type and variety.
Eating: as soon as possible after picking.

Blackcurrants
Harvesting: early part of mid-summer to late summer, depending on the variety.
Eating: as soon as possible after picking.

Red and white currants
Harvesting: early part of mid-summer to late summer, depending on the variety.
Eating: as soon as possible after picking.

Gooseberries
Harvesting: latter part of early summer to the early part of late summer, depending on the variety.
Eating: as soon as possible after picking.

Raspberries
Harvesting: early part of mid-summer to mid-autumn, depending on the type and variety.
Eating: as soon as possible after picking.

Blackberries
Harvesting: late summer to the latter part of early autumn, depending on the variety.
Eating: as soon as possible after picking.

Hybrid berries
Harvesting: mid-summer to the early part of mid-autumn, depending on the type.
Eating: as soon as possible after picking.

Strawberry

Blackcurrant

Gooseberry

Raspberry

Lawn choices

Is grass the only option?

Most medium to large gardens have a lawn, formed either by sowing seeds or laying turves, although in many warm countries inserting tufts of grass into a surface is considered best, especially for small areas. In subtropical regions, a mixture of grass cuttings and moist soil spread over the surface produces good results if kept moist until well established. Chamomile and thyme are other choices, although they are not hardwearing and are mainly decorative.

WHAT DO GRASS LAWNS DO FOR GARDENS?

Well manicured lawns form traditional parts of gardens, creating playing areas for toddlers and sports-active youngsters, as well as unifying a garden and creating a framework for other garden features. Indeed, if well designed they can lead the eye to areas which, at first glance, are not apparent.

Lawns need not be flat – they can create terraces, be formed into steep banks or gentle slopes – and can be bounded by regular, irregular or curved edges.

INFORMAL   FORMAL

SEED OR TURVES?

Each of these methods of creating a lawn has advantages and disadvantages:

Advantages with seed:

- Cheaper than laying turves.

- Easy to create intricately shaped areas.

- Lighter work than laying turves.

- Once the area has been prepared and the seed bought, you do not have to commence sowing immediately – bad weather or lack of time to sow seed within a few weeks does not create problems. However, it may be necessary to rake the surface again if children or pets have trodden on it.

- The range of lawn seed is wide and it is easy to select the type of grass suited to the area and the expected wear.

Turf

Disadvantages with seed:

- After sowing and germination, it is necessary to wait 3–4 months for the grass to become fully established before the surface can be used.

- If the area is not well prepared, perennial grasses can be a problem before the fine ones are established.

- Protect the seed from birds by covering the entire area with wire-netting, which is an expense and a nuisance. Alternatively, black cotton can be strung 10–20 cm (6–8 in) above the surface, but not harm birds.

- Cats tend to dig up newly sown soil; toddlers and young children are invariably lured to the area.

Advantages with turves:

- Creates an instant sward, but will take up to four weeks before it can be used.

  - Eliminates problems created by birds and cats.

  - Ideal where there are young children who might disturb the surface of a newly sown lawn.

  - Turves can be laid at almost any time from spring to autumn (though irrigation must be provided during dry periods).

Disadvantages with turves:

- More expensive than sowing seeds.

- Turves have to be laid within 24 hours of delivery. If left, exposed sides begin to dry and the grass becomes yellow.

- It involves much heavier work than when sowing seeds.

Whatever the shape or style of a garden, a lawn unites the entire area. In formal gardens the lawn needs to be cut more regularly than in less regimented areas, especially when used by youngsters as a sports area.

CHAMOMILE LAWNS

Lawns formed of *Chamaemelum nobile* (Chamomile; earlier known as *Anthemis nobilis*), a prostrate, mat-forming herbaceous perennial, are very unusual. Plants have finely dissected leaves which when bruised and walked on release a fruit-like bouquet. However, it is the non-flowering form 'Treneague' that is more widely used to create lawns, with a fragrance resembling that of bananas. Chamomile lawns are more for decoration than daily use.

THYME LAWNS

Thymus serpyllum (English or Wild Thyme) can be used to create a decorative lawn-like feature where hard wear is not a consideration. Plants are near prostrate, carpet-forming and with richly fragrant, grey-green leaves, with flowers ranging in colour from white to pink and red. Stepping areas, formed of paving or sections of tree trunks, help to ensure that wear to plants is limited.

Using containers

Growing plants in containers has achieved a near cult status. Choose from windowboxes, wall-baskets and hanging-baskets (suspended from wall-brackets) that bring colour to windows and walls. Plants suitable for containers range from relatively permanent ones, such as shrubs, trees and conifers, to seasonal types like summer-flowering bedding plants and tender foliage plants that survive outdoors in summer, but need warmth in winter.

Why should I use containers?

RANGE OF CONTAINERS

Windowboxes

↗ Structure: range of sizes, but inner plastic troughs about 82 cm (32 in) long, 20 cm (8 in) wide and 18 cm (7 in) deep are easily handled, and these can be placed inside outer windowboxes with an ornate nature.
Display period: by having three separate inner plastic troughs ('spring', 'summer' and 'winter' displays) they can be seasonally rotated within the outer windowbox.

Hanging-baskets

↗ Structure: range of sizes and materials; wire-frame baskets range in widths from 25 to 50 cm (10–20 in), and about half as deep.
Display period: mainly summer when outdoors, but if in lobbies and conservatories their display is longer, especially when planted with foliage and flowering houseplants.

Wall-baskets and mangers

→ Structure: range of materials, including wire-framework; wide metal strips (mangers); plastic and terracotta. Manger-types are 30–72 cm (12–28 in) wide; wire-frame ones 23–50 cm (9–20 in) wide; plastic and terracotta types 15–25 cm (6–10 in) wide.
Display period: usually during spring and throughout summer.

Tubs

↗ Structure: wood (either specifically constructed as tubs or barrels cut in half). Ensure that they are strong.
Display period: throughout the year when containing a shrub, tree or conifer. Also, summer-flowering bedding plants, spring-flowering bulbs, herbaceous perennials and climbers.

Troughs

↘ Structure: range of sizes and materials, from those that resemble windowboxes and constructed of plastic, glass-fibre or wood, to ornate stone types.
Display period: spring, summer and winter, depending on the plants.

Urns

Structure: stone is the traditional material, but also plastic, glass-fibre and reconstituted stone.
Display period: throughout the year, but influenced by the type of plants that are used.

Stone sinks

Structure: traditional sinks are shallow stone types earlier used in kitchens. Additionally, sinks can be home-made by using a mixture of cement powder, sharp sand and fine peat. They are not difficult to make.
Display period: throughout the year when planted with a medley of diminutive rock garden plants, alpines and small, spring-flowering bulbs. Miniature conifers can also be used.

Styles of garden

A garden can be whatever you choose it to be and most are a medley of several different styles, with particularly desired features added to it. An all-weather patio or terrace is important, with a durable lawn for games and leisure, around which other garden features can be created. Greenhouses, rock gardens and water features are particular favourites. You must also be prepared to remodel your garden as your family grows up, and demands on it change.

Is there a wide choice?

GARDEN STYLES TO CONSIDER

Formal or informal

In earlier years, gardens were often classified as either formal or informal; formal types are regimented in nature, with clinically shaped beds and borders, while informal ones have a relaxed and less strict aura. Harmonizing the garden's style with the house is important, especially when considering the front garden. Too often, when moving into a new property, the car takes priority and concreting the area appears to be an imperative (see page 31 for practical yet inspirational ideas).

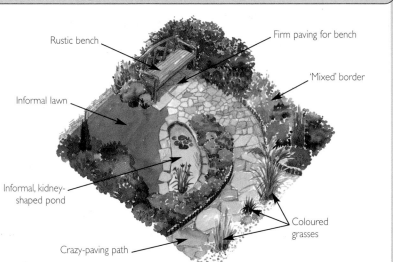

Rustic bench

Informal lawn

Informal, kidney-shaped pond

Crazy-paving path

Firm paving for bench

'Mixed' border

Coloured grasses

↗ *Informal gardens have a more relaxed and casual nature than formal and regimented types (see below).*

↗ *Always ensure that the garden reflects the design nature of the house, whether with a modern or earlier structure.*

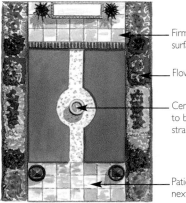

Firm, all-weather surface

Flower beds

Central feature to break up long, straight lines

Patio immediately next to house

↗ *This design exudes formality, with rigid lines that soon take the eye right to the end of the garden, where an additional leisure area has been created.*

GARDEN STYLES TO CONSIDER (CONTINUED)

Patios and containers

➔ This style appeals to many gardeners, especially where the area is small, perhaps irregularly shaped, the soil impoverished or the land excessively steep and unworkable unless terraced. Many plants, from summer-flowering bedding plants to shrubs, trees and conifers, can be grown in containers, but daily attention is essential, especially when the weather is warm.

Balcony gardening

➔ Container gardening is ideal for balconies, where they can be used to cloak stark edges at the bases of balustrades, brighten walls and extend the living area. Tubs and pots of slightly tender plants are a possibility, especially as in winter they can be taken inside.

Courtyard gardening

↙ Courtyards are enclosed on all sides by walls, thereby secluded and protected from strong winds. Being enclosed, they are often shaded and using shade-loving plants is essential. However, they can create superb gardens in small and often inhospitable areas.

Cottage gardens

➔ These are informal, and consist of a medley of flowering plants, vegetables, herbs and fruit.

LOW- AND EASY-MAINTENANCE GARDENS

There are subtle differences between 'low-maintenance' and 'easy-maintenance' gardens, although the reasoning can often be a little blurred.

• An easy-maintenance garden is a lawn – and little else! All that is then needed is to cut the grass weekly, from spring to autumn; this is often ideal for young families where ball games and bicycles take priority.

• A low-maintenance garden is one where the area is planned to have desirable features and plants, yet requires minimal maintenance.

• Even very large gardens can have an 'easy-maintenance' nature when mainly formed of lawns and where efficient lawn mowers and edging equipment are used.

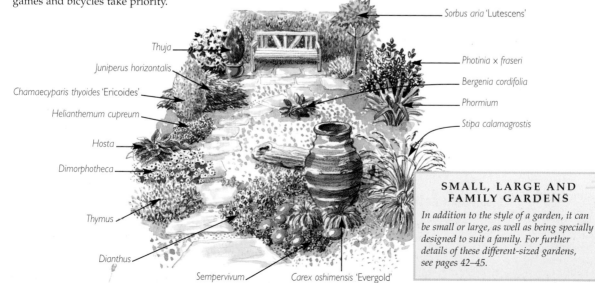

Thuja

Juniperus horizontalis

Chamaecyparis thyoides 'Ericoides'

Helianthemum cupreum

Hosta

Dimorphotheca

Thymus

Dianthus

Sempervivum

Carex oshimensis 'Evergold'

Sorbus aria 'Lutescens'

Photinia × fraseri

Bergenia cordifolia

Phormium

Stipa calamagrostis

SMALL, LARGE AND FAMILY GARDENS

In addition to the style of a garden, it can be small or large, as well as being specially designed to suit a family. For further details of these different-sized gardens, see pages 42–45.

Tools you will need

Do I need many tools?

A range of well-made garden tools that suits your height and build is an investment for life, and will make gardening far more enjoyable and easy than badly made tools that are heavy and difficult to handle. Always buy the best-quality tools you can afford: stainless-steel types are expensive and durable, but others are just as long-lasting if cleaned after use and stored in a dry, well-ventilated shed. Tools can be grouped into several main types.

ESSENTIAL GARDENING TOOLS

For first-time gardeners there are a few general tools that are immediately needed, such as:
• Spade (see right)
• Fork (see right)
• Iron rake (see page 15)
• Dutch hoe (see page 15)
However, the need for specific tools is invariably dictated by the state of the garden. For example, if hedges and lawns have been neglected, powered equipment is essential in order to bring the garden under control. This section of the book details all the tools you are likely to need.

LOOKING AFTER TOOLS

Regular care extends the life of garden tools:
• After every use, wash metal and wooden parts in clean water, and thoroughly dry.
• Wipe bright-metal parts with a cloth coated in light oil.
• Clean wood or plastic handles and wipe dry.
• Oil bearings and other moving parts.
• Store in a dry, airy shed, with hand tools hanging from hooks so that lower ends do not trail on the floor. With lawn mowers, park them on strips of wood.

CHECK BEFORE BUYING

Before buying any tool, whether a spade, hoe or secateurs, always check that it is easy to handle and is a pleasure to use. Spades and forks that are too heavy or large will be a continual problem. With secateurs, check that the handles do not open too wide and cause strain to small hands.

Spade and fork handles

There are three types of handle, and it is a matter of personal preference which you choose (check the feel of them before buying).

T-shaped   *D-shaped*   *D-Y outline*

DIGGING AND FORKING TOOLS

Garden spades

Mainly used to dig soil in autumn and winter, although they are useful throughout the year for jobs such as moving soil and trimming lawn edges (if you do not have an edging-knife or edging-iron). Spades are made in several sizes:
• **Digging types:** blades about 27 cm (11 in) long and 19 cm (7½ in) wide.
• **Border types:** often sold as 'lady's spades', they have blades 23 cm (9 in) long and 14 cm (5½ in) wide.
Some spades have blades with tread-like ledges at the top of the blade, and this enables more foot pressure to be used when digging heavy, clay-like soil. However, they are heavier to use and more difficult to clean than those that have a straight blade.

Spade

   Most spades are sold with 72 cm (28 in) long handles (the distance from the top of the blade to the tip of the handle), although some are 82 cm (32 in).

Garden forks

Often used to dig extremely heavy clay soil in winter, as well as shallowly scarifying surface soil in spring and summer in shrub borders and between herbaceous plants. They are also ideal for breaking down large lumps of soil in spring when you are preparing ground for sowing or planting. There are several types and sizes:
• **Digging forks:** often known as garden forks, these have four prongs (tines), each 27 cm (11 in) long.
• **Border forks:** these also have four prongs, but only 23 cm (9 in) long.
• **Potato forks:** these are similar to digging types, but with flat rather than round prongs. This helps to prevent tubers being damaged while being harvested (lifted) from the soil.

Fork

HOEING TOOLS

Hoes are used to cultivate the soil's surface, severing weeds and creating friable soil on the surface. There are several types.

Draw hoes

These have a goose-neck-shaped head that angles a sharp-edged blade back and towards the user; the head is attached to a 1.5 m (5 ft) long wood or plastic handle. Draw hoes are mainly used to form shallow drills when sowing seeds, as well as for severing weeds at ground level. They can also be used to form 15 cm (6 in) deep drills when planting potato tubers.

When forming a drill, walk backwards, drawing the hoe's head towards you; when using the hoe to remove weeds, move forwards.

Dutch hoes

Formed of a wood or plastic handle, about 1.5 m (5 ft) long, attached to a 10–15 cm (4–6 in) wide, flat piece of metal, sharpened on its leading edge, a Dutch hoe is ideal for severing weeds at ground level and for forming a tilth that helps to reduce loss of moisture from the soil. To use one, walk backwards, systematically pushing the blade forwards through the soil.

Draw hoe   *Dutch hoe*

Onion hoes

These resemble miniature draw hoes, with a 7.5 cm (3 in) wide blade secured through a goose-neck head to a wood or plastic handle, 30–38 cm (12–15 in) long. They are used to sever weeds around seedlings, and to create a tilth.

RAKING TOOLS

Essential for levelling soil, removing debris from borders and lawns, and preparing ground for sowing lawn seed and laying turves. There are several types.

Iron rakes

Most popular type and ideal for removing debris from the soil's surface. They have 25–30 cm (10–12 in) heads, with 10–14 teeth, each 6–7.5 cm (2½–3 in) long. The head is fitted to a wood or plastic hand, 1.5 m (5 ft) long.

Landscape rakes

Useful for levelling large areas of soil, often in preparation for sowing lawn seed or laying turves. They have a 72 cm (28 in) wide wooden head, with 7.5 cm (3 in) long tines spaced about 36 mm (1½ in) apart.

Rake

MEASURING TOOLS

Measuring rods

A piece of wood, 1.5–1.8 m (5–6 ft) long and 5 cm (2 in) wide and about 18 mm (¾ in) thick. Along one side are lines shallowly cut into the surface, spaced about 7.5 cm (3 in) apart.

Garden lines

Garden lines

At its most basic, a garden line is a strong piece of string attached at each end to a piece of wood that can be inserted into the ground. Some garden lines, however, have a metal spike at one end, and a rotating device at the other that enables string to be wound around it.

PLANTING TOOLS

Hand trowels

Formed of a shallow metal scoop, with a handle 15–30 cm (6–12 in) long; ideal for planting small plants.

Hand forks

Similar in size to trowels, with a head formed of 3–4 metal tines. They are ideal for digging out shallowly rooted weeds and for cultivating surface soil.

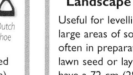
Hand trowel   *Hand fork*

Dibbers (dibbles)

Simple tools, used for making planting holes in vegetable plots or in seed-trays (flats). In gardens they are used to plant cabbages, cauliflowers and other brassicas, as well as leeks. They are 30–38 cm (12–15 in) long, but usually become worn down through use. Small dibbers/dibbles (like thick pencils, but shorter) are used in greenhouses when transferring seedlings to wider spacings in pots and seed-trays (flats).

Bulb planters

Useful when planting bulbs in grass; you can use them to remove a core of soil and turf. Then place a bulb in the base of the hole and replace the soil and turf over the top of it.

Dibber

Pruning tools

How much equipment will I need?

Strong secateurs that make clean cuts are essential for pruning shrubs, roses and thin stems on trees, fruit bushes and canes. For branches and thick stems, however, saws are essential. Long-handled secateurs, sometimes known as loppers, are ideal for cutting thick stems, especially those at the centre of a dense, prickly shrub. Hedges need sharp garden shears, or powered hedge-trimmers if the hedge is large. Always use powered tools with great care.

Safety with chainsaws

When cutting off a large branch or cutting down a tree, chainsaws are invaluable – but take extreme care when using them.

- *Keep children and domestic pets indoors.*
- *Do not use during wet weather.*
- *If electrical, use a power-breaker in the circuit to ensure safety if the cable is cut.*
- *Wear goggles, strong gloves and a jacket.*
- *Do not wear a scarf or necktie.*
- *Have an assistant with you.*
- *Do not stand on a box or ladder.*
- *Do not use above waist height.*

TOOLS AND EQUIPMENT

Secateurs *For general pruning*

These are available in two basic forms. The bypass type (also known as parrot or cross-over) has a scissor-like action and cuts when one blade passes the other. The anvil type has a sharp blade that cuts when in contact with a firm, metal surface known as an anvil. Both cut well, but must not be strained in cutting thick shoots.

Bypass secateurs

Anvil secateurs

RIGHT- OR LEFT-HANDED?

Most secateurs are for right-handed gardeners, but left-handed types are available and these make pruning an easier and more pleasant job for 'lefties'. These secateurs allow the cutting positions of the blades to be more easily seen, and therefore the risk of damage to buds is reduced.

Long-handle secateurs *For out-of-easy-reach shoots*

Also known as long-handled loppers, these have the same cutting actions as secateurs – bypass and anvil. Most of them have handles 38–45 cm (15–18 in) long and cut wood up to 3.5 cm (1½ in) thick. Heavy-duty types have handles 75 cm (2½ ft) long and cut wood 5 cm (2 in) thick. Additionally, some have a compound cutting action that enables thick branches to be cut with very little physical effort.

Bypass long-handle secateurs

Anvil long-handle secateurs

Garden shears and powered hedge-trimmers

Garden shears are ideal for trimming hedges and beds of heathers. Ensure that they open and close easily, cut cleanly and do not unnecessarily jolt hands and wrists. Where a hedge is large, powered trimmers make life easier. Most are driven by mains electricity, some by petrol-powered generators (ideal in areas far away from a power supply), while others are cordless and cut about 83 sq m (100 sq yds) between charges.

Cutting blades range from 33 to 75 cm (13–30 in) in length. Some have cutting knives on one side only; others have them on both sides.

Garden shears

Electric hedge-trimmer

High-reach electric hedge-trimmer

TOOLS AND EQUIPMENT (CONTINUED)

Saws for all purposes   *For cutting branches of all sizes*

Folding saws are usually 18 cm (7 in) long when folded and extend to 40 cm (16 in). They cut on both the push and pull strokes, severing wood 3.5 cm (1½ in) thick. Straight-bladed saws with fixed handles cut branches about 13 cm (5 in) thick, while Grecian types have curved and pointed blades and cut on the pull stroke. They are ideal for cutting branches in awkward positions. Bow saws are 60–90 cm (2–3 ft) long, with a blade kept under tension by a lever. They are ideal for cutting thick branches.

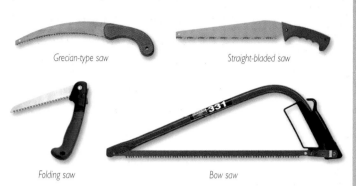

Grecian-type saw

Straight-bladed saw

Folding saw

Bow saw

Pruning knives
For experienced gardeners only

Knives have been used to prune plants for many decades, but their use is best reserved for gardeners with practical experience of them. They must be very sharp, and in the hands of a novice can be a lethal weapon. Therefore, they are best reserved for smoothing the surfaces and edges of large cuts on trees before an application of a wound paint. Take care when using a knife.

Pruning knife

High-reach pruners
For safety-first pruning

Also known as branch or tree loppers, these enable high branches to be pruned while the pruner stands safely on the ground. They cut shoots 2.5 cm (1 in) thick at heights up to 3 m (10 ft). They are ideal for pruning large and vigorous fruit trees.

High-reach pruners

Gloves and kneeling pads
When pruning roses

Stout but flexible gloves prevent hands being ripped by thorns, while a kneeling pad makes bush roses easier to reach. Kneelers are also useful as their side supports help infirm gardeners to get down and up easily without back strain.

Kneeling pad

Gloves

Knee pads

Buying good tools

It is false economy to buy a poor-quality gardening tool as it will soon fail and may harm you, especially if a powered type. In addition, sharp-edged tools may soon lose their sharpness. Therefore, always buy a reputable brand from an established store.

Hiring tools

Many gardening tools can be hired, but usually it is those that are only occasionally needed, such as chainsaws. Before hiring a chainsaw, confirm that it is in good condition, with a sharp chain and bottle of lubricating oil.

TOOL MAINTENANCE

Pruning tools must be kept sharp and in good condition if they are to operate and function easily and properly.

- Wash and wipe tools after use and coat bright surfaces with thin oil, especially if stored for several months.

- Chains on chainsaws need frequent checking during use, but first unplug the power cable.

- Check power cables at the end of each season and replace those that are damaged.

- Store equipment in an airy, waterproof shed. If it is slightly damp, wrap small tools in a dry cloth and place in a polythene bag.

GETTING A GRIP

Before buying a gardening tool, always handle it to ensure that it feels right for you. Pruning tools – especially secateurs – should be comfortable to hold and easy to use. If too large for your hand, it is difficult to put the desired pressure on the handles. If too small, there is a chance of fingers being pinched when handles are closed.

Check loppers to ensure that the handles, as the blades close and cut, do not nip and trap large hands.

When testing garden shears, check that as they cut they do not jolt your hands and wrists; some shears have rubber stops to prevent this happening. Additionally, check that the shears cut along their entire cutting edges.

Lawn tools

Do I need many tools?

Clearly, a lawn mower is essential and there is a wide range of them, from hand-pushed to ride-on types. The type of mower you need depends on the size of the lawn and the desired neatness of the cut (a range of mowers and the surfaces they create is shown on pages 20–21). The powered types are usually driven by mains electricity (with a safety device fitted into the circuit) or by a petrol engine. Rakes, edging tools and lawn aerators are also needed.

RAKING AND BRUSHING TOOLS

There are plenty of garden tools for keeping lawn surfaces smart, and these include:

Spring-tined rake

Plastic-tined rake

Spring-tined rakes

Fan-like heads, about 50 cm (20 in) wide, formed of wire tines. They are ideal for raking lawns to remove leaves and dead grass.

Plastic-tined rakes

A variation on the spring-tined type, but instead of wire tines they have plastic ones. Heads fan out to about 60 cm (2 ft) wide.

Rubber lawn rakes

Ideal for removing dead grass and scattering wormcasts. Formed of a wood or plastic handle, about 1.5 m (5 ft) long, and a 45 cm (18 in) wide head with about 33 flexible rubber tines. Some heads are 30 cm (1 ft) wide, with 18 rubber tines.

Besom

Formed of brush-like twiggy stems firmly secured to a handle about 90 cm (3 ft) long. It is a traditional brush and used to sweep up debris as well as to brush and scatter wormcasts.

AERATING TOOLS

Well-aerated lawns encourage the healthy growth of lawn grasses. There are several ways to achieve this:

Garden fork

On a small lawn, insert the prongs of a garden fork about 10 cm (4 in) deep into the turf, spacing each line of holes 13–15 cm (5–6 in) apart.

Hollow-tine fork

Foot-operated, with three hollow tines that remove cores of turf; the ensuing holes must have fresh soil brushed into them. Do not use this tool on the same piece of turf more frequently than every 3–4 years.

Solid-tine aerator

Wheeled and hand-pushed, with solid spikes being pushed into the soil. Can be difficult to operate on heavy and dry lawns.

Slitter aerator

Wheeled and hand-pushed, with rotating, sharp-edged discs, spaced about 5 cm (2 in) apart, being forced to slice through surface soil. There are also electric and petrol-powered types.

Slitter aerator

FERTILIZER SPREADERS

It is always possible to spread lawn fertilizers by hand, but for novice gardeners it is better to use a fertilizer spreader that ensures even and correct distribution. Most distributors are two-wheeled, with adjustable mechanism enabling the correct amount of fertilizer to be spread over the lawn's surface.

LAWN SWEEPERS

During autumn and into early winter, lawns often become covered in fallen leaves. They can be swept up with lawn rakes and besoms, but mechanical lawn sweepers help to make this task easier, especially if the area is large. There are also electric and petrol-powered tools that suck up leaves.

Lawn sweeper

WEED-KILLING EQUIPMENT

Lawn weeds can be tackled in several ways:
- Pulling up by hand or by using a small, pointed trowel; if there are not many of them, this is the best method (roots are easily pulled from the ground after a shower of rain).
- Using a wheeled distributor (but thoroughly clean afterwards).
- Using strings to systematically mark the lawn into metre or yard strips, and to use a watering-can fitted with a dribble bar to evenly water the surface. Mark the watering-can with an X and keep it solely for weed-killing chemicals.

STRIMMERS

These are ideal for cutting long grass around trees and alongside paving. There are electric, petrol- and battery-powered types.

Strimmer

Safety-first with electricity

Never use a mains-powered lawn mower, strimmer or other tool without ensuring that a Residual Current Device (RCD) is fitted in the circuit. Sometimes, it is known as Ground Fault Circuit Interrupter (GFCI). These ensure that, should a cable be severed, the electricity is immediately cut off. Additionally, always use cables that are recommended for use outdoors, rather than indoors. Store these cables in a dry, well-ventilated garage or shed.

TRIMMING AND EDGING TOOLS

Cutting and trimming tools need special care to ensure that sharpened edges are not blunted. Clean and dry bright surfaces after use, and thinly coat in light oil.

Edging knives

Earlier known as edging irons and half-moon edging irons, they are sharpened on their lower and rounded edges and used to cut lawn edges. The head is fitted to a handle about 90 cm (3 ft) long.

Edging shears

Formed of a pair of metal or wood handles, about 82 cm (32 in) long, fitted to two blades, each 18–20 cm (7–8 in) long. By opening and closing the handles, you can trim grass at the edges of lawns.

Hand shears

Used to trim long grass as well as to cut hedges. It is normally necessary to kneel or bend down when using them, but long-handled shears enable grass to be cut without having to stoop.

Edging knife

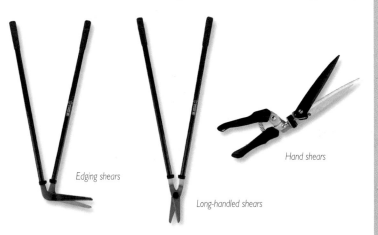

Edging shears

Hand shears

Long-handled shears

Short-handed lawn shears

Ideal for cutting long grass around trees, on narrow banks or for trimming grass on seats formed of grass. They are hand-operated, with spring-loaded short blades, and can be operated with one hand.

Nylon-cord edging trimmers

Several horizontal strimmers can be adjusted to a vertical position so that they cut long grass along the edges of lawns.

Lawn mowers

Is a lawn mower essential?

A mower is necessary to keep a lawn neat and tidy, cutting the grass 12 mm (½ in) to 30 mm (1¼ in) high from early spring to mid-autumn. However, global warming may eventually mean that lawns need to be cut throughout the year, but not so short. Usually, cutting a lawn once a week is all that is needed, but in summer – when grass is growing quickly – it is often necessary to mow twice a week. Most mowers have grass-collection boxes.

TYPES OF LAWN MOWERS

Some 50 or so years ago, most lawn mowers were hand-pushed. Nowadays, most are powered by electricity or petrol. Most are guided by hand, but some are ride-on vehicles and are ideal for very large lawns.

Hand-pushed cylinder mowers
Single cylinder, usually with 5–6 blades that cut against a sharp, bottom plate. For an extra fine cut, machines with 8–12 blades are needed (often used on bowling greens). The blades are normally driven by a split roller at the back of the machine, although earlier ones with side wheels were popular and cheaper, but more likely to slip on wet grass. Cutting widths are 25–40 cm (10–16 in).

Powered cylinder mowers
Single cylinder, driven by electricity or petrol. Lightweight electrical types have 30–35 cm (12–14 in) cutting widths, while petrol-driven types have 30–106 cm (12–42 in). For a small to average-sized lawn, an electrical mower is ideal, whereas for large areas a petrol type is more robust and practical; petrol storage can be a problem, however.

Rotary mowers
The body of the mower is mounted on four small wheels, with a sharp-edged blade rotating horizontally slightly above the lawn's surface. The height of the blade can be adjusted. Electrically driven types have 25–45 cm (10–18 in) wide cutting areas, while petrol-powered ones are slightly more robust and larger with 35–75 cm (14–30 in) cutting widths. Both of these types of mowers are pushed over the lawn and are not power-driven.

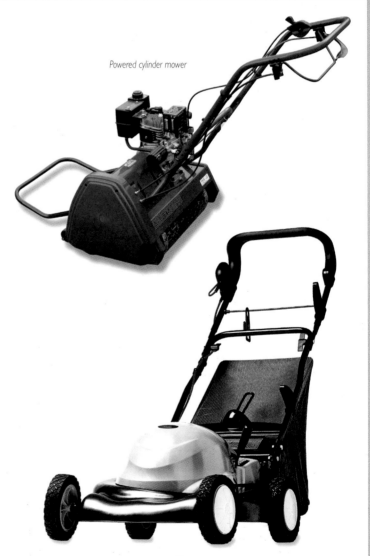

Powered cylinder mower

Rotary mower

TYPES OF LAWN MOWERS (CONTINUED)

Hover mowers

Powdered either electrically or by a petrol engine, a sharp-edged blade rotates horizontally above the lawn, on a cushion of air. The height of the cutting blade can be adjusted. They have cutting widths of 25–45 cm (10–18 in). These are ideal for cutting grass on banks, as well as over stepping stone in lawns. There is a range of models and some have grass collection boxes.

Ride-on mowers

Only practical for large lawns; there are two main types:

- Cylinder machines with a trailing seat and petrol powered. Widths of the cutting cylinder are 53–75 cm (21–30 in), and most have a grass-collection box. They are easy to steer and turn in small areas.
- Tractor-type mowers are petrol-driven, with a rotating horizontal blade to cut the grass. Cutting height is adjustable. This type also has a grass-collection box and the way it cuts makes it ideal for use on long grass.

Undercover storage is essential for ride-on mowers, as well as for all other types. It may be necessary to make a moveable ramp to enable a ride-on mower to be taken into a large, raised shed; ensure that the flooring is strong. Usually, there is no problem about driving a ride-on type into a garage.

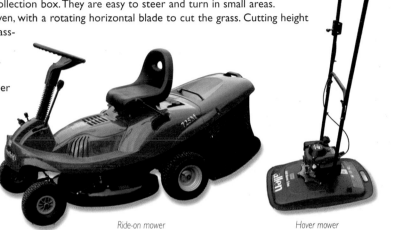

Ride-on mower

Hover mower

ELECTRICAL OR PETROL-DRIVEN?

Each type has its devotees and here are a few considerations for each of them:

Electrically powered mowers

- Quieter than petrol-driven mowers, and the noise instantly stops when the machine is at rest.
- Must have a power-breaker (Residual Power Device) fitted into the power socket, with the socket for the mower's cable plugged into it. Should the cable become severed by the mower's blades, the power-breaker causes the power supply to be immediately cut off before the user can be harmed. Never mow a lawn unless this device is installed.
- Ideal where frequent rest periods are needed during the mower's use.
- Cable length up to 60 m (200 ft), and if cables are joined ensure moisture-proof fittings are used.
- Do not use in wet conditions.
- Usually cheaper to buy than an equivalently powered petrol engine.
- Does not entail the storage of petrol.

Petrol-driven mowers

- More robust than electric types.
- No risk of running over and severing a cable.
- Depending on the size and power, cuts tall grass more easily than electric types.
- Demands a safe and secure storage shed for cans (not plastic bottles) of petrol.

CHOOSING THE RIGHT SIZE OF MOWER

The time it takes to mow a lawn is critical, and although a mower with a narrow cutting width will, eventually, cut even the largest area, there is a 'best width' theory (see below) that enables a lawn to be cut within 30 minutes. Also beware of buying a too large and difficult-to-handle mower to cut a small lawn.

Here is a guide to selecting a mower's cutting width.

Lawn area	Cutting width of mower
450 sq m (530 sq yd)	30 cm (12 in/1 ft)
650 sq m (770 sq yd)	35 cm (14 in)
850 sq m (1,000 sq yd)	40 cm (16 in)
1,050 sq m (1,250 sq yd)	45 cm (18 in)
1,250 sq m (1,500 sq yd)	60 cm (24 in/2 ft)

Creating stripes on lawns

Few lawns are as attractive as those with parallel stripes formed of alternate bands of light and dark green grass. These stripes are the width of the mower's back roller; only mowers with a roller construction will create them. Ensure the stripes are straight and equal in width. Before mowing a lawn and creating stripes, use the mower to cut two strips at each end.

Cultivating and assessing soil

What is soil?

Soil is a complex and continually changing mixture of mineral particles, air and water, and animals and plants in varying stages of decay. There are also soil organisms (from microscopic fungi and bacteria that break down complex compounds to simple ones that plants can absorb) to worms that play an important part in the soil's aeration and the distribution of organic material. The mineral part is formed of fine and coarse sand, clay and silt.

HOW TO ASSESS YOUR SOIL

Digging the soil in winter and leaving it ridged creates a friable surface for sowing seeds in spring.

Organic material

Water

Clay

Silt

Light sand

Coarse sand

Stones

After filling a screw-top jar with a soil sample and water (see below left), tighten the lid, shake the jar and allow the mixture to settle.

There are several ways to judge if a soil's composition is light, medium or heavy:

- Pick up a small amount of soil and rub it between your forefinger and thumb. If it has a smooth and slippery feel, the soil contains a high proportion of clay. If it feels gritty, however, then it is predominantly sandy.
- Fill a screw-top jar a quarter to half full of soil, then add tap water until it is three-quarters full. Shake vigorously for a few minutes, then place on a table and allow to settle for half an hour. It will form layers – stones at the bottom, then coarse and light sand, followed by silt and clay. Organic material will float on the surface. The proportions of these layers indicate the predominant nature of the soil.
- Although not scientific, the 'boot' test is infallible. Walk over the soil in winter when it is wet – if it contains a high proportion of clay, it will lovingly stick to your boots. Incidentally, clay is not necessarily acid, so you will need to assess its pH before adding lime (see page 23).

INTERPRETING THE RESULTS

- **If predominantly clay:** these soils are heavy and notoriously difficult to work, slow to warm up in spring and likely to become cracked and baked in summer. However, their small clay particles retain plant foods better than sandy types. They are often badly drained and land drainage is usually necessary (see pages 24–25). There are clay particles in most soils and it is only when they form more than 35 per cent of the total soil that problems arise.

- **If mainly formed of silt:** these particles are slightly larger than clay, but smaller than those of sand. In general, silty soils are poorly drained and lack the chemical-retentive qualities of clay; they also tend to be acid in nature. After a rain shower the surface also forms a cap and prevents the entry of air.

- **If highly sandy:** these soils are light, well-drained and warm up early in spring (ideal for growing early salad crops). Unfortunately, plant foods are quickly leached away and the digging in of bulky organic materials (farmyard manure and garden compost) is essential. Mulching the soil is also important (see page 27).

SOIL ACIDITY AND ALKALINITY

The acidity or alkalinity of soil plays an important part in growing plants; most plants grow in a pH of 6.5–7.0, which is slightly acid to neutral. The pH scale ranges from 0 to 14, with figures below 7.0 indicating increasing acidity, and those above greater alkalinity. There are two good ways to assess soil:

- Most lime-testing kits use chemicals that when mixed with soil and water produce a colour reaction which can be compared with a colour chart, thereby indicating the pH value.
- More recent is a piece of equipment with a probe that is inserted into the soil and the pH reading shows on a dial. This is ideal for gardeners who are red-green colour-blind.

A few pH soil testers have a probe that you just insert into the soil, and are very easy to use.

Decreasing the alkalinity of soil

This is more difficult than counteracting acid soil, and is best achieved by annually digging in plenty of farmyard manure and garden compost, and through the use of acidic fertilizers such as sulphate of ammonia. Alternatively, grow plants in neutral soil in raised beds, or select only lime-loving plants. Growing plants in containers is another solution.

Decreasing the acidity of soil

Apply lime immediately after winter digging: the amount required depends on the degree of acidity, type of soil and the form of lime used (see below).

Some pH soil testers depend on the comparison of colours, and can be harder to use.

TO MAKE YOUR SOIL MORE ALKALINE

The amounts of lime required to decrease acidity by 1.0 pH (aim for a pH of about 6.5).

SOIL	HYDRATED LIME	GROUND LIMESTONE
Clay	610 g sq m (18 oz sq yd)	810 g sq m (24 oz sq yd)
Loam	410 g sq m (12 oz sq yd)	540 g sq m (16 oz sq yd)
Sand	200 g sq m (6 oz sq yd)	270 g sq m (8 oz sq yd)

Soil-type indicators

Some native plants (often erroneously known as weeds) indicate the nature of soil, especially if it has never previously been cultivated. These include:

Poor, infertile soils
- *Briza media* (Quaking Grass)
- *Holcus lanatus* (Soft Creeping Grass, Yorkshire Fog)
- *Rumex acetosella* (Sheep's Sorrel)
- *Senecio jacobaea* (Ragwort)

Damp, heavy soils
- *Cardamine pratensis* (Lady's Smock)
- *Carex* spp. (Sedges)
- *Equisetum* spp. (Horsetails)
- *Juncus* spp. (Rushes)
- *Lychnis flos-cuculi* (Ragged Robin)
- Mosses (some)
- *Ranunculus repens* (Creeping Buttercup)
- *Tussilago farfara* (Coltsfoot)

Good, loamy soils
- *Ranunculus* spp. (Buttercups)
- *Senecio vulgaris* (Groundsel)
- *Sonchus arvensis* (Sow Thistle)
- *Stellaria media* (Chickweed)
- *Taraxacum officinale* (Dandelion)
- *Urtica* spp. (Stinging Nettles)

Chalky soils
- *Centaurea scabiosa* (Greater Knapweed)
- *Cichorium intybus* (Chicory)
- *Echium vulgare* (Viper's Bugloss)
- *Fumaria officinalis* (Fumitory)
- *Linaria vulgaris* (Yellow Toadflax)
- *Pimpinella saxifraga* (Burnet, Salad Burnet)
- *Silene vulgaris* (Bladder Campion)

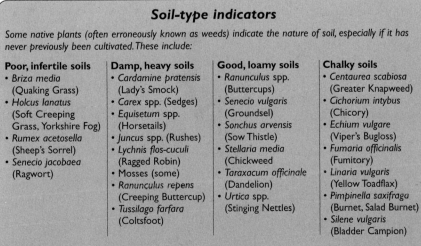

AIR, WATER AND SOIL

Both air and water are vital for the growth of plants, but the nature of a soil influences their availability.

- **Water:** this is essential for the growth of plants; clay soils remain wetter than sandy types, but are reluctant to release moisture to plants.

- **Air:** this is vital for the growth of roots and the existence of many beneficial soil organisms. Sandy soils are better aerated than heavy, clay types.

Drainage

Why is this important?

Although a few plants thrive in wet soil, most require conditions where excess water readily drains away, leaving moisture-retentive soil that is well aerated. Both roots and many soil organisms breathe and if deprived of air soon decay; eventually, the soil becomes inert and smelly. Conversely, if soil is mainly formed of sand and too well drained it dries out rapidly in summer and plant growth decreases. Ways to install land drains are explained here.

IDENTIFYING BAD DRAINAGE

If water continually remains on the soil's surface, it is clear that drains are required. Rushes and reeds are other indications of excessive soil moisture. Another test is digging a hole about 90 cm (3 ft) deep in autumn and monitoring the level of water in it throughout winter. If water remains within 23 cm (9 in) of the surface for long periods, drains are required (see below for details of the types and their installation). Cover the hole to prevent children falling in.

DRAINING OPTIONS

Clay pipe drains

This is the traditional way to drain soil and involves laying a line of unglazed, clay pipes. They are about 30 cm (1 ft) long and for main drains those with a bore of 10 cm (4 in) are best, with 7.5 cm (3 in) for side drains. They are laid in trenches and on shingle, in the same way as for corrugated plastic drains (see right).

Rubble drains

➔ Relatively inexpensive and quick to install, especially if you have a ready source of clean rubble or large pebbles. Form main and side drains in the same way as for perforated plastic and clay pipe drains, and fill the trench to about half full with clean rubble or large pebbles. Then, spread several layers of thick polythene over the top to prevent the rubble becoming clogged with debris: cover and firm with topsoil.

Soakaways and ditches

➔ One problem when draining soil is to where the water should be channelled. The solution is either a soakaway, or a ditch or stream bordering the garden.
• Ditch or stream: few gardeners have this option, but if you do just allow the pipe to protrude about 10 cm (4 in) from the bank and cover the end with small-mesh wire-netting to prevent vermin entering it.
• Constructing a soakaway: position a soakaway at the lowest position. Dig a hole about 1.2 m (4 ft) square and with its base about 30 cm (1 ft) below the pipe that directs water into it. Fill the hole to about half its depth with clean rubble, then to within 30 cm (1 ft) of the surface with shingle. Cover this with double-thickness strong polythene and top up with topsoil. Initially, leave the soil mounded, as it invariably settles.

Rubble drain

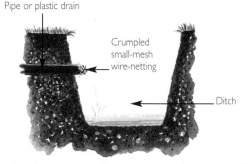

Side drain · Main drain · Rubble · Several layers of thick polythene · Drainage trench

Rubble drains are inexpensive if plenty of clean rubble and pebbles are available.

Drainage into a ditch

Pipe or plastic drain · Crumpled small-mesh wire-netting · Ditch

If present, a ditch is an easy way for water to escape from water-saturated soil.

DRAINING OPTIONS (CONTINUED)

Installing plastic drains

You will need rolls of perforated, corrugated, 10 cm (4 in) or 7.5 cm (3 in) bore tubing that is usually bought in rolls 25 m (82 ft) long. This is laid in trenches with at least a 1-in-90 decline towards a sump or outlet into a ditch or stream.

1 *Dig a main trench with a uniform, 1-in-90 decline towards a sump or outlet into a ditch or stream. Dig trenches 60–75 cm (24–30 in) deep and 30–45 cm (12–18 in) wide. Side drains are needed, spaced 3.6–4.5 m (12–15 ft) apart for heavy clay soils and 7.5–9 m (25–30 ft) for sandy types. Before digging, use strings to mark the positions of the main and side drains.*

2 *Ensure that the trench has a uniform slope; remove all loose soil from the base. Spread a 5 cm (2 in) thick layer of shingle in the base of the trench, and place the perforated plastic tubing on top. Check that the tubing is in the centre of the trench and is straight.*

3 *Where a side drain meets the main drain, cut its end so that it closely fits against the side of the main pipe. There is no need to cut the main drain. Cover the joint with two layers of strong polythene to prevent gravel falling into the pipe.*

4 *Spread a 7.5–10 cm (3–4 in) thick, uniform layer of shingle over the pipes. Cover the shingle with a double thickness of strong polythene to prevent soil contaminating it and, eventually, blocking the drainage system. Add and firm topsoil. Leave the soil slightly mounded, as later it will settle.*

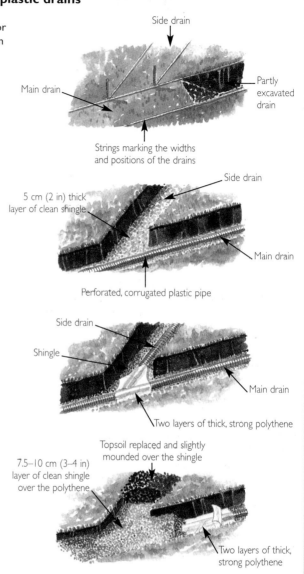

Side drain

Main drain

Partly excavated drain

Strings marking the widths and positions of the drains

5 cm (2 in) thick layer of clean shingle

Side drain

Main drain

Perforated, corrugated plastic pipe

Side drain

Shingle

Main drain

Two layers of thick, strong polythene

Topsoil replaced and slightly mounded over the shingle

7.5–10 cm (3–4 in) layer of clean shingle over the polythene

Two layers of thick, strong polythene

After laying drains

- After laying drains, replace topsoil (not sub-soil) in the trench.

- Firm the soil by treading over it; then, form it into a slight and continuous mound. During the following months, this will settle and be level with the surrounding soil.

- If the drains run through an established lawn, either sow seeds (spring or early autumn) or lay turf (mid- or late spring, but better in autumn).

RAISED BEDS

Where the installation of drains is not possible (perhaps because there is no convenient outlet for the drainage water, or the garden is exceptionally small) raised beds are a solution to the problem.

- Ensure that the walls surrounding the bed are strongly constructed and with a firm base.

- When preparing the bed, dig down to about 23 cm (9 in) and spread a thick layer of clean rubble over the base. Then, replace the topsoil.

Digging

Annually digging garden soil in winter helps to improve its aeration and drainage, as well as giving plant roots easier access and keeping the area free from weeds. While digging, decayed manure and garden compost can be mixed in with the soil to add nutrients and to improve its structure. Digging soil in the winter and exposing the larvae of soil pests, such as cockchafers, leatherjackets and wireworms, to frost and birds, helps in their control.

Why dig the soil?

BENEFITS OF DIGGING

Although many plants often appear to grow well for many years in land which is not cultivated, these are usually grasses and native flowers in meadows. However, in gardens either initial soil cultivation (before long-term plants such as shrubs and trees are planted, or lawns sown or created from turves) is essential, as well as yearly cultivation when vegetables are grown. These are the benefits of winter digging in preparation for growing plants:

- Inverts the top layer of soil, burying annual weeds (perennial ones are best dug up and destroyed, as if parts are left they re-grow during the following spring and summer). Never put them on a compost heap.
- Enables well-decayed farmyard manure and garden compost to be mixed with soil while digging proceeds.
- Improves drainage and aeration and ensures that the surface soil allows rain to enter the soil. Surfaces of some soils form a crust, which unless disturbed prevents water and air entering.
- Exposes the larvae of soil pests to frost and birds.
- Loosens soil, making it easy for seeds to germinate and roots to grow.
- Exposes the surface to the soil-breaking activities of frost, snow, wind, rain and sunshine. This creates a friable surface for the sowing of seeds in spring.

Is it practical not to dig?

The practicality of adopting a no-digging policy is influenced by the soil's make-up. On most soils, especially clay types, digging the soil is the best policy. On light and sandy soil, and where perennial weeds are not a problem, it is possible to grow crops, mainly vegetables, on the top of compost regularly placed on the soil's surface.

Devotees of this method claim that is it a natural way to grow plants, but many gardeners have difficulty in buying the necessary well-decomposed manure and garden compost each year.

SINGLE AND DOUBLE DIGGING

Single digging

Divide the plot down the middle of its length. Take out one 'spit' or 'trench' – the depth and width of the spade – from the first half and lay the soil down on one side. Add manure or compost to the trench bottom. Remove the thin layer of weeds from the second trench and lay it upside-down in the first trench. Take out the soil from the second trench to the depth of one spit and lay it over the weeds in the first trench. Repeat the procedure down to the end of the plot. Move to the second half and continue. When you get to the end of the second half, put the contents of the first spit that you dug into the last trench.

Double digging

Divide the plot down the middle of its length. Take out two 'spits' (see left) – so as to finish up with a trench about 60 cm (2 ft) wide – and lay the soil down on one side. Add manure or compost to the trench bottom and turn it over to the full depth of a fork. Skim the turf about 5 cm (2 in) deep from the next two spits and lay it upside-down in the first trench. Take out the soil from the next two spits and lay it over the turf so as to fill up the first trench. Repeat the procedure down to the end of the plot. Continue on the second half. At the end, put the contents of the first two spits that you dug into the last trench.

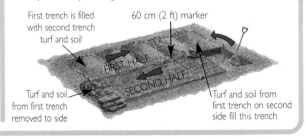

Soil from first trench is removed to the other side (this will fill the final trench)

FIRST HALF

SECOND HALF

Soil from first trench on second half fills last trench on first half

First trench is filled with second trench turf and soil

60 cm (2 ft) marker

FIRST HALF

SECOND HALF

Turf and soil from first trench removed to side

Turf and soil from first trench on second side fill this trench

Conserving soil moisture

It is becoming increasingly important to try to retain moisture in the soil as much as possible during hot, dry spells. This can be achieved in two ways: by keeping the area free from weeds, which deprive plants of both moisture and plant foods, and may be harbingers of pests and diseases; and by mulching – many materials, from well-decomposed manure and garden compost to plastic sheeting and shingle, can be used as a mulch.

How can I prevent moisture loss?

ORGANIC MULCHING MATERIALS

Most of these are derived from decayed plants that are spread over the soil's surface (but not touching plants) to about 7.5 cm (3 in) deep. Before applying a mulch, check that the soil is moist and free from perennial weeds. Possible organic mulches include:

- **Farmyard manure:** increasingly difficult to obtain and best dug into the soil during winter, especially if it is not fully decomposed. It contains a wide range of plant foods (major, minor and trace elements) and therefore as well as conserving soil moisture helps in the long-term and healthy growth of plants.
- **Garden compost:** created by systematically forming kitchen and soft-plant waste from garden plants into layers in a compost heap. When fully decomposed (about six months in winter, but only three in summer) it can be used as a mulch or for digging into the soil. Incidentally, when fully decomposed it is friable, brown and sweet-smelling.
- **Peat:** frequently recommended as a mulch, but as it is extracted from peat beds it results in the destruction of the natural habitats of many animals, birds and insects. Therefore, using it as a mulch is environmentally unfriendly. In any case, unless kept moist it is soon blown about by wind and disturbed by birds.
- **Bark chippings:** create an effective mulch and especially useful in ornamental gardens for spreading around shrubs and trees. Unfortunately, because the chippings are light, birds invariably disturb them when seeking grubs in the damp soil beneath the mulch.

- **Wood chippings:** formed of chopped woody waste, such as stems and twigs, and ideal as an inexpensive home-made mulch. Electrically powered shredders can be bought or hired and woody garden waste converted into chippings. Unfortunately, like bark chippings it is easily disturbed by birds and strong wind, although it decomposes more rapidly.
- **Grass cuttings:** can be either composted (best way) or applied fresh around plants. However, when used directly from a lawn, ensure that the turf has not recently been treated with a weedkiller. Form a mulch only 2.5 cm (1 in) thick and keep it away from the stems of plants. This is because as it decomposes it warms up; it may also attract slugs and snails, causing damage to plants.
- **Straw:** sometimes used as a mulch, especially around strawberry plants where it keeps the fruits dry and prevents heavy rain storms splashing soil on them. Unfortunately, the straw blows about and does not readily decay. Also, considerable bacterial action is needed to break down its structure, often leading to nitrogen deficiency in the soil.

Non-organic mulches

These do not add nutrients to the soil, but just suppress the growth of weeds and keep the ground moist.

Black polythene: increasingly used to suppress the growth of weeds and to conserve soil moisture, especially when growing strawberries. When used to mulch strawberries, form a 15–20 cm (5–8 in) high and 45 cm (18 in) wide mound of soil, water it (but not excessively), and stretch a strip of black polythene about 60 cm (2 ft) wide over it, with the edges held in place by being inserted into 7.5 cm (3 in) deep slits. Cut star-like slits, 38–45 cm (15–18 in) apart, along the top and put strawberry plants in them. Carefully firm soil around the roots and fold back the polythene.

Shingle: pea-shingle mulches around rock-garden plants help to keep the soil moist, preventing the growth of weeds and stopping muddy soil splashing on plants. They also reduce the activities of slugs and snails.

HOEING

Using a Dutch hoe or draw hoe to sever weeds at ground level and to create a fine tilth helps reduce moisture loss from the surface of the soil.

Trenches

Starting plants off in trenches helps to conserve moisture around their roots, as well as enabling you easily to blanch (see page 74) the stems of some vegetables by returning soil to the trench as they grow. Celery is sometimes grown in this way.

Tropical ploy

In the tropics, coconuts were sometimes sown in holes 90 cm (3 ft) deep and square, where the soil was moist. One nut was placed in each hole and, initially, only a small amount of soil mixed with decomposed manure placed over it.

Exposed gardens

Are exposed sites a problem?

Such gardens are a disadvantage when trying to grow crops that are sown or mature early, are tall and at risk from being buffeted by strong winds, or flower when there is still a risk from late-spring frosts. It is possible to reduce the velocity and damaging effects of wind by planting windbreaks or hedges, as well as installing fencing that diminishes the wind's speed without causing dramatic and plant-damaging turbulence on the lee side.

REDUCING THE WIND'S SPEED

The wind's speed is dramatically reduced on the sheltered side (see below)

Hedges and windbreaks diminish the wind's speed and make life more congenial for plants.

Windbreaks and tall hedges help to create a plant-friendly garden, where strong and cold winds are not a problem. Position the windbreak or hedge – formed of hardy evergreen conifers or deciduous trees – on the windward side of the garden.

The influence of a windbreak or hedge depends on its height. Where it is 6 m (20 ft) high, you can expect it to reduce the wind's speed by 65 per cent at a distance of five times its height, but by only 15 per cent at a distance of 20 times its height.

IS FROST A PROBLEM?

It is especially damaging to plants with young, tender stems, shoots and flowers, such as summer-flowering bedding plants, and to fruit trees that flower early in the year and therefore have blossom that is at risk.

PROTECTING TENDER BEDDING PLANTS

- Where late frost is known to be a problem, keep plants in a greenhouse or conservatory until all risk of frost and the damage it can cause has passed.
- If plants have been put in containers, such as windowboxes and hanging-baskets, and there is an unexpected risk of frost, place 2–3 layers of newspaper over them at night.

PROTECTING FRUIT TREES

- In cold areas, where late frosts are a problem, select those fruits and varieties that flower later and therefore are not at such risk. For example, pears are more sensitive to frost than apples, as the blossom appears 2–4 weeks earlier
- If a frost is unexpected, spray the blossom with a fine misting of clean water before the frost starts to thaw. This raises the temperature around blossom and helps to prevent damage.

PROTECTING TENDER SHRUBS

Some shrubs growing in tubs are damaged by frost and cold wind. Plants can be protected by inserting five canes, about 1.5 m (5 ft) long, into the compost at the edges of the tub and forming them into a wigwam. Wrap straw around them and secure with a spiral of string. Remove as soon as all risk of frost has passed.

Insert several canes into the compost and form them into a wigwam.

Clothe them in straw and hold in place with a spiral of string.

Avoiding frost pockets

Air frost naturally travels downhill. Therefore:

- Do not grow frost-susceptible plants at the bases of slopes.

- Do not plant a tall hedge across a slope, as it prevents frost escaping, thereby creating an area of frost and putting at risk plants trapped there.

- When gardening on a slope, do not plant espalier or cordon tree fruits across the slope. Neither should you plant cane fruits, such as raspberries, across the slope.

Dealing with slopes

Slopes can be both a problem and opportunity. Clearly, moving from one part of a slope to another is more difficult than when on a flat surface, and during torrential rainstorms water may rush off the surface and wash away soil. Slopes are also more expensive to develop than a flat site. However, a slope offers opportunities to create an unusual garden, with a series of paved, terraced areas. Grass banks are possible and these are inexpensive ways to link terraces.

Are slopes a problem?

TOP OR BOTTOM OF A SLOPE?

When a house is at the bottom of a facing slope:
- A wide, flat, paved area is essential between the base of a slope and the house, together with provision for rapidly draining rainwater that may rush down the slope.
- A paved area about one-third of the way up the slope helps to break up the often visually daunting nature of a slope, as well as creating an area of relaxation.

When a house is at the top of a slope:
- Construct a flat, paved area as near to the house as possible, with meandering paths leading downwards from it, perhaps crisscrossing the slope to make them less steep and easier to use.
- Paved areas do not have to be central. This especially suits informal gardens.

RETAINING WALLS

These are invariably constructed across slopes to retain banks of soil up to 1.2 m (4 ft) high. Some walls are formal, while others are made of natural stone, with small gaps to enable plants such as aubrietia and *Aurinia saxatilis* (still better known as *Alyssum saxatile*), to be planted in them. Position a wide path at the side of an informal wall to prevent plants growing in them being damaged when people walk by.

Always ensure that the wall has weeping holes, through which water can drain. If this is neglected, the pressure of water in the ground will eventually topple the wall.

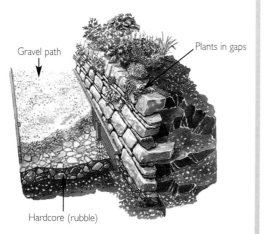

Gravel path

Plants in gaps

Hardcore (rubble)

Some retaining walls are 'battered' (they slightly lean backwards to help retain the soil).

LAWN BANKS AND STEPS

Traditionally, and especially on large country estates, slopes were terraced and grassed, with 45° slopes separating 3–3.6 m (10–12 ft) wide level areas. These dramatic features can be replicated on a smaller scale in formal gardens; steps can be cut into the bank.

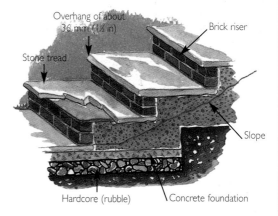

Overhang of about 36 mm (1½ in)

Brick riser

Stone tread

Slope

Hardcore (rubble)

Concrete foundation

Position each 'tread' so that it slightly slopes towards the overhang at the tread's edge.

SLOPING WOODLAND AND WILD GARDENS

Old railway sleepers are ideal for retaining soil on steep slopes in rustic areas. Secure the sleepers in position, using strong wooden posts or metal spikes. Beds of heathers and deciduous azaleas create superb displays on slopes.

Creating privacy

Privacy in a garden is increasingly important, both within the garden itself and to reduce the possibility of being overlooked by neighbours. Tall boundary hedges that provide screening and diminish excessive road noise are not always possible, and apart from creating shade they result in impoverished and dry soil along the hedge's base. Trellises, screens, pergolas, gazebos and arbours are constructional features which produce seclusion as well as privacy.

TRELLISES, PERGOLAS, GAZEBOS, ARBOURS AND ARCHES

Trellises

➔ Roses and flowering climbers (see pages 58–9 for screening plants) create feasts of colour – often with fragrance – on trellis screens.

How to make a small lean-to pergola

➔ Construct a small, lean-to pergola against a wall to create a plant-covered leisure area. Concrete the base of each vertical post in a 60 cm (2 ft) deep hole. Secure cross-timbers (beams) to wall-brackets (anchors); a traditional, formal design is best. Use a builder's spirit-level (carpenter's level) to check that the posts are upright and the main beam is level.

Strong, main beam
Secure ends to wall with joint hangers
Cross-beam
Strengthening corner pieces
Concrete base into ground
Slope top of concrete
Strong wooden post

Gazebos

➔ With a long heritage and a name meaning 'to gaze out', gazebos are distinctive garden features, especially when positioned to have a wide vantage point. Ramblers, with their relaxed habit and massed flowers, are ideal for clambering over and decorating gazebos.

Arbour

➔ Self-assembled or ready-made arbours can be used to create attractive focal points at the end of a garden quickly and simply.

↗ *Jasminum officinale* (Common White Jasmine) forms an attractive partnership with the light and dark blue flowers of *Clematis macropetala* and deep purple-blue flowers of *Lavandula* 'Hidcote'.

Arches

➔ Add an Oriental quality to the top of an arch by chamfering or ornately shaping the lower ends of the cross-timbers (beams). The ends of these timbers (beams) should protrude 23–30 cm (9–12 in) from the arch's sides.

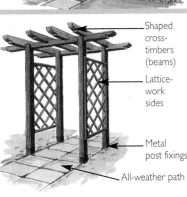

Shaped cross-timbers (beams)
Lattice-work sides
Metal post fixings
All-weather path

Keeping cars off the road

Increasingly, front gardens which earlier were solely filled with ornamental plants are being redesigned to enable cars to be parked off-road. Even gardens with a drive that could accommodate a single car now have flower beds changed into firm surfaces for a second car. Unless care is taken when converting a front garden, it can be as aesthetically pleasing as a tarmac-covered car park; but this unsightly spectacle can be avoided.

How do I convert my front garden?

CONSTRUCTION FACTORS

- Whatever the type of area being converted, its design must harmonize with the house.
- Water drainage from a large, hard-surfaced area is often a problem and care must be taken not to direct it to the foundations of houses or, worse, through air-bricks near the bases of walls or above damp-proof courses. Also, avoid draining it into garages!
- Gravel and shingle are excellent bases and they especially harmonize with older properties. They also have the advantage of enabling water to drain through to the subsoil. However, do not use shingle and gravel if there is a radical slope away from the property, as they will migrate on to the pavement and road.
- If the area is very narrow and cars cannot be turned around, turntables are available; this avoids having to back out onto a busy road.

- If a hard standing area is needed for only 3–4 years, choose paving slabs, concrete pavers (used for flexible paving) or gravel, which can be easily and cheaply removed if you wish to re-establish a 'proper' garden. Before engaging a construction company to install a standing area, ask if it can be easily and inexpensively removed.
- Ensure that access is still possible to water stop-taps and drainage covers.

GARDEN AESTHETICS

- If possible, leave an area for a lawn and flower beds. Even the smallest lawn brings life and colour to an area.
- Where a small bed next to a house is possible, plant climbers and wall shrubs. Doorways especially benefit from an arch and added flower colour.
- If no space is left for flower beds, use windowboxes, hanging-baskets, troughs and tubs.

HOW TO CREATE A PARKING GARDEN

Order of work
- Draw your design, including the house, the boundaries, drains, immovable structures and any large trees.
- Mark out the parking area.
- Dig the area out to a depth of 30 cm (1 ft).
- Set the edging in concrete.
- Put down well-compacted rubble and top it off with bricks bedded in sand – or concrete if the ground is soft.

Planting
Include plants like dwarf conifers and slow-growing alpines – the type of plant that you would normally grow in a rockery or scree bed. Place hanging baskets or containers at the side of the door.

Remember ...
It may be necessary to gain permission from your local planning authority before converting a front garden into a car-parking area. Changing a kerb to a slope may also require permission.

Choosing a path

Whatever a garden's size, an all-weather path is essential; it needs to be a fundamental part of a garden's design and not something added as an afterthought. Paths enable easy access to functional features, such as sheds and greenhouses, as well as to more ornamental designs such as summerhouses, gazebos and pergolas. The range of surfaces and material is wide. Some have a rustic charm, while formal ones are better for modern houses and gardens.

Is a garden path necessary?

PATH ESSENTIALS

Apart from having an all-weather surface, the design of a path should:
• unite all parts of a garden;
• create a visual perspective, so that the eye is not confused and has a known feature to travel along;
• introduce style, whether formal or informal; and
• be individualist and unique, creating originality.

Slopes and paths to avoid

Some materials are not suitable for slopes, or where the surface is undulating.

Paths to avoid on a slope are those:
• formed of gravel or pea shingle that spills on to other areas;
• with large paving slabs that would, at their joints, be uneven; and
• formed of flexible pavers laid on a bed of sharp sand.

RANGE OF PATHS

There is a great variety of path materials and many ways to use them. Below are many inspirational designs. Some are suitable for informal gardens, whereas others are more clinical and formal. Always select a style that harmonizes with your garden planting and does not confuse the eye.

↗ *Gravel paths edged with lavender are ideal for an informal garden.*

↗ *Paving slabs in several sizes help to create a semi-formal path.*

↗ *Bricks or pavers in a herringbone pattern look tidy and attractive.*

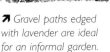

↗ *Complex patterns using paving slabs and bricks give an exotic touch.*

↗ *Crazy paving is suitable for a relaxed garden atmosphere.*

↗ *Ribbed-surface concrete paths are slip resistant and easy to build.*

↗ *Coloured setts can be laid in complex and intricate patterns in an ornate garden.*

↗ *Bricks laid crossways may look attractive but they are not very strong.*

↗ *Use stone chippings for rustic paths, edging them to retain the stones.*

↗ *Old pieces of paving introduce an informal style to a garden.*

↗ *Wooden strips with pea gravel between them are very eye-catching.*

CORNERS, CURVES AND STEPS

When selecting a path, always consider whether materials used in its construction are able to cope with curves. Some materials, such as square paving slabs, are best used on straight paths, whereas crazy paving is suitable for both straight and curved areas.

PATH EDGING

Edgings formed of log rolls or bricks set at an angle are ideal for curved paths, whereas concrete edging slabs and bricks when laid flat are difficult to negotiate around a curve. Some edgings can be used to abut a lawn, but side constraints are essential where a path is formed of gravel.

Creating a brand new garden

Starting with a 'greenfield' site, possibly with a new-build house, is an opportunity rarely available to first-time gardeners, and a neglected garden is the nearest to a virgin site that you will normally get. Reclaiming a derelict garden is a mystery tour – occasionally, plants such as bulbs reappear from beneath the undergrowth, while shrubs may still be present. However, if the area has been neglected for more than ten years, they are usually not worth keeping.

Where do I begin?

ASSESSING THE AREA AND SOIL

Before clutching your spade and marching boldly into the proposed garden, full of excitement and anticipation about creating the garden of your choice, take some time to assess its attributes, such as orientation, the soil and whether the site has a radical slope. Although it may appear to be time-consuming and wasteful, sketching out the garden on scaled paper and marking in permanent features, as well as trees you may wish to retain, helps to forge practical solutions to problems that may arise.

A perspective view of the garden is more difficult to draw than a plan view, but is nevertheless the best way to visualize your design. Important features can be drawn separately and in more detail.

ORIENTATION

Mark the position of the house, as well as trees you may wish to retain, on scaled paper. Stand in the garden at various times of the day and assess the sun and its shadows. Decide, for example, if you want a patio in full sun, or a vegetable plot in full sun yet out of sight of the house. If possible, carry out this assessment of the sun and its shadows for several months, as the difference between high summer and winter can change dramatically. Remember, too, that with the possibility of stronger and longer summer sun, shade may become more important than having sunlight.

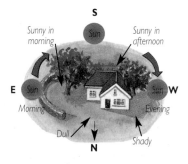

Design the garden so that it makes the most of the sun.

Make a note of your neighbour's house, its orientation and position, since there is a question of needing privacy from it. Achieving privacy in a garden is featured on page 30, as well as pages 58–59.

EXPOSED SITES

Ordinary garden plants dislike strong wind, which can deform them (especially before they are fully established) as well as causing them to absorb increasing amounts of moisture from the soil to compensate for that transpired by leaves. There may be natural windbreaks already present in the garden, perhaps created by a neighbouring house, your house as well as sheds, fences and walls. However, remember that solid barriers create strong eddies of wind and that hedges are a better solution for creating a more plant-friendly garden (see page 28).

SLOPING GROUND

This need not be a problem and can even add character and interest to a garden, although invariably it is more difficult, time-consuming and costly to design and maintain a sloping garden. For ways to overcome these problems, see page 29.

SOIL TYPES

Usually, the nature of the soil in the garden is the last consideration when buying a new property, and all soil types create opportunities and problems. Excessively wet land can be drained (see pages 24–25), and soil samples can be analysed to see if it is predominantly formed of clay, silt or sand (see page 22). Assessing the acidity or alkalinity of soil is also featured on page 23; by the way, it is easier to correct excessive acidity than alkalinity, where raised beds and growing chalk-loving plants may be the solution.

Conserving moisture in the soil is increasingly important, and ways to achieve this are featured on page 27.

Tailoring your garden

Whatever the nature of the site or soil, it is essential to plan the garden to suit your entire family, although it will invariably change as children age. Family gardens are covered on page 42, and play and leisure areas on page 3. Many other gardening opportunities, from growing ornamental plants to producing your own food, are featured throughout this book.

Formal gardens

These gardens are regimented, often with beds, borders and lawns that have uniform, straight or regularly curved outlines. Sometimes there are narrow flower beds alongside lawns, filled throughout summer with summer-flowering bedding plants. Border edging plants, such as *Lobularia maritima* (Sweet Alyssum, and *Lobelia erinus* (Edging Lobelia), are frequently interplanted with *Salvia splendens* (Scarlet Sage), which introduces scarlet flowers to the display.

The red bricks, pergola and close-cropped lawns have a formal nature.

Symmetrical designs have an open and dignified appearance that appeals to many gardeners.

Psychological influence of formal gardens

Formally shaped gardens have clinical, geometric lines that keep thoughts in regimented compartments. They are also said to concentrate the mind, directing and confirming beliefs.

Demand on time

Regular attention is needed, especially to mow lawns and to trim their edges. When grass is left uncut and edges allowed to become straggly, the entire area soon loses its regimented look and appears unkempt, neglected and lacking any design purpose.

CARPET BEDDING

During the mid-1800s, many low-growing, subtropical plants were introduced into temperate gardens, and within a decade were grown to form decorative carpets of colour in flower beds. Most were planted in geometric patterns and a legacy of this can still be seen in many parks, coastal towns and cities. In gardens, this often transposed to lines of *Lobularia maritima* inter-spersed with lobelia, with foliage plants such as *Abutilon pictum* 'Thompsonii' and *Bassia scoparia* 'Trichophylla' (Summer Cypress; also known as *Kochia scoparia* 'Trichophylla') used to introduce dots of height to the display.

SPRING-FLOWERING DISPLAYS

As soon as summer-flowering bedding plants lose their colourful displays in late summer or early autumn, they are removed, the bed dug and biennial plants and spring-flowering bulbs such as tulips planted. Biennials include *Dianthus barbatus* (Sweet Williams) and *Erysimum cheiri* (Wallflower; also known as *Cheiranthus cheiri*).

KNOT GARDENS

Now mainly formed of *Buxus sempervirens* 'Suffruticosa' (Dwarf Edging Box), but earlier of many other plants including *Thymus* spp. (Thyme) and *Hyssopus* spp. (Hyssop), knot gardens were an expression of the unchanging, endless nature of life. By the mid-1600s, the knot garden became a term for a flower garden surrounded and interwoven with formal paths. Today, knot gardens are usually formal edgings to borders and alongside paths.

TOPIARY

The art of shaping shrubs and trees by training and regularly clipping them into symmetrical shapes for formal gardens and, amusingly, into depictions of birds and animals for informal gardens is known as topiary. Cones, spheres, squares, pyramids, spirals and tiered cones are best in formal surroundings.

Many different plants are used to create topiary, including the slow-growing *Taxus baccata* (Yew), *Buxus sempervirens* (Common Box) and *Lonicera nitida* (Chinese Honeysuckle).

FORMAL PONDS

Round, square or rectangular ponds are ideal for formal gardens. They can be positioned in many places, including on patios and terraces. Alternatively, set them in the centre of a wide lawn, and partly surrounded by formal paths and flower beds. Raised ponds, with their sides 45–60 cm (18–24 in) high, create distinctive features. Fountains, with symmetrically shaped columns or sprays of water, can be added.

Formal water gardens can become central features in a garden.

Informal gardens

These have a more relaxed and casual feel than formal gardens, with irregularly shaped beds and borders. They are not as relaxed as cottage gardens (see page 36), which include a diverse medley of vegetables, fruits and ornamental plants in the same border, but nevertheless have a restful ambience. It is a readily adaptive style of gardening; whereas with formal gardens it may be difficult later to alter and add other features, with informal ones it is easy.

What are informal gardens?

Informal gardens have an easy-going character that encourages relaxation, reflection and contemplation.

Psychological influence of informal gardens

The controlled informality creates a friendly and restful ambience. It is also likely to encourage more birds into a garden than a formal design, thereby extending the range of stimulating yet restful sounds.

Demand on time

Although borders and lawns need attention from spring to autumn, if time is limited or the weather unsuitable for gardening for a few days or a week, it will not be too disastrous; but mow lawns and trim their edges as soon as possible.

HERBACEOUS BORDERS

Herbaceous plants produce a feast of colour throughout summer and into early autumn. Plants have life-spans of 3–4 years before they become congested and need to be dug up and divided; replant young pieces from around the outside of the clump and discard the old and woody central part. Some of these plants are self-supporting, while others need support from twiggy brushwood or several canes with garden wire or string tied around them. Proprietary supports are also available. Most herbaceous plants are grown in borders with only one viewing side. However, the self-supporting types can be grown in 'island borders' positioned in large lawns. Where possible, make a kidney-shaped island bed, no more than 1.8–2.4 m (6–8 ft) wide; this enables you to reach the plants without having to tread on the border.

MIXED BORDERS

These have an informal appearance, and are formed of a medley of herbaceous perennials, shrubs and trees, with gaps filled with spring- and summer-flowering bulbs, biennials, hardy annuals (sown where they flower) and summer-flowering bedding plants (earlier raised in gentle warmth in late winter and early spring, for later planting into a garden when all risk of frost has passed). Although a mixed border is a medley of different plants, it needs careful planning to ensure that heights and colours vary and that the border does not appear to be regimentally tiered from front to back.

Mixed borders are inevitable in small gardens, where space is limited.

SOOTHING SOUNDS

Wind chimes suspended from trees and close to a house add a gentle, relaxed and comforting sound to a garden. However, do not position them where they may cause irritation through being repeatedly knocked.

INFORMAL PATHS

Rather than having paths in straight lines and constructed of formal paving or pavers, those in informal gardens can meander and be formed of informal materials – even gravel and grass with stepping stones set in them. Crazy paving and rustic bricks create visually relaxed paths. Paths created from *Thymus* spp. (Thyme) or *Chamaemelum nobile* (Chamomile; also known as *Anthemis nobilis*), with stepping stones, are other considerations.

INFORMAL PONDS

These have a relaxed outline, with construction from flexible liners, rigid liners and concrete. They can be fitted into corners close to a house. However, avoid totally shaded areas, or under trees where, in autumn, leaves would fall into the water.

Cottage gardens

What are cottage gardens?

These have an even more relaxed character than informal gardens (see page 35), with medleys of vegetables, culinary herbs, fruits and ornamental plants often in the same border or just separated by stepping-stone paths. In the front gardens of cottage-style houses you can use gravel as a standing area for cars and screen it off with a trellis of roses, *Lonicera* spp. (Honeysuckle) and *Humulus lupulus* 'Aureus' (Yellow-leaved Hop), with Rosemary.

Few styles of gardening gain as much attention as a cottage garden, with its rich medley of different plants.

Water-pump barrels introduce a nostalgic yet practical feature to a cottage garden.

This distinctive arbour introduces a romantic ambience to cottage gardens.

Psychological influence of cottage gardens

Cottage gardens have a casual and informal nature that encourages relaxation and friendliness. They reduce stress and inspire philosophical thoughts; they are also considered to have a healing quality derived from their informality yet constant need to be nurtured to maintain their relaxed and distinctive ambience.

Demand on time

Because cottage gardens are a medley of plants, they need regular attention, not just to keep them tidy but also to ensure that each plant is not intruding too far on its neighbour's territory. This is especially necessary in early summer, when plants are growing quickly, and from the latter part of mid-summer to early autumn, when many vegetables and fruits are ready to be harvested.

BUTTERFLY AND BEE GARDENS

Attracting butterflies and bees into a cottage garden adds vitality and further interest. Bees produce a distinctive buzz and, unless threatened, seldom sting, instead happily going about their task to collect nectar and pollinate flowers. Butterflies are becoming rarer and many gardeners endeavour to create butterfly-friendly gardens. Plants that encourage butterflies include *Buddleja davidii* (Butterfly Bush), *Lavandula* spp. (Lavender), *Sedum* 'Autumn Joy', *Phlox paniculata* (Perennial Phlox) and *Mentha spicata* (Spearmint).

Incidentally, avoid white-flowered plants as they do not attract bees or butterflies. Preferably, choose a sunny, wind-sheltered site, and do not use chemical sprays when bees are active. Keeping a diary of when specific butterflies are first seen helps to create further interest in the garden.

TOPIARY

Symmetrically shaped topiary suits formal gardens, whereas those clipped to the shapes of birds or animals are better in cottage gardens. Their basic shapes are created around wire frameworks, with regular clipping and pinching out of shoots to produce a detailed figure; this process will take several years.

RUNNER-BEAN TRIPODS

Runner beans are often grown to clamber up rows of beanpoles or string netting, when they can be used to create colourful screens as well as edible pods when 15–20 cm (6–8 in) long, mainly during late summer and into early autumn. However, in cottage gardens they are also superb when grown up poles that form tripods 1.8–2.1 m (6–7 ft) high. These can be installed among vegetables and between ornamental plants.

RUSTIC TRELLISES

Rustic-pole trellises are superb when clothed in roses and *Lonicera* spp. (Honeysuckle) and are ideal as backdrops for cottage gardens. They also introduce privacy to gardens.

FENCES FOR COTTAGE GARDENS

White picket fencing has a clinical look, while wattle hurdles create an ideal background for informal plants. Ensure that the individual hurdles are well secured to strong posts. As well as being used as boundary fences, low hurdles are excellent as temporary screens within cottage gardens, where they can be positioned to protect young plants from strong winds.

Patio and courtyard gardens

Increasingly – and especially on patios (see page 40), in courtyards and on terraces – growing plants in containers is popular, with hanging-baskets, windowboxes and tubs bursting with colour. Some containers can be filled with colour throughout the year, and others solely in summer. Their displays are versatile and clothe not only patios, courtyards and terraces, but also walls, windows, verandahs, balconies and pergolas (see pages 38–39).

How do I grow the plants?

PATIO, COURTYARD OR TERRACE?

Much confusion has arisen about 'sitting-out' areas in gardens, especially as house agents prefer upmarket terms and call any hard surface a patio.

- **Patio:** we owe this term to the Spanish, who used it to describe an inner courtyard surrounded by the dwelling and open to the sky. In hot climates, this provides shade and shelter throughout the day.
- **Courtyard:** these have a long history and were used over 1,000 years ago in Islamic forts, palaces and religious buildings, where they created shady areas out of direct sunlight. However, today's courtyards, mainly in town gardens, are usually small, secluded and protected from strong wind.
- **Terrace:** correctly, this is an open, all-weather surface at the rear of a house, connecting the garden with the house. If raised above the general level of the garden, it may have a balustrade or low wall along its garden side.

STORAGE AND WORKING AREAS

A clean storage area for pots, tubs and composts is essential; it can also be used to store containers when not in use. If you wish to raise your own plants as well, rather than buying from garden centres or nurseries, a heated greenhouse – or a shed with large windows – will be essential in late winter and early spring.

WATER SUPPLY

An accessible supply of clean water is essential; do not rely on water stored in water-butts, which has probably drained off a roof and may be

Overhead screens help to create further privacy.

Cosy and closeted areas are ideal as extended living extensions to homes. Screens soon make them more private areas.

Plants in containers enable displays to be quickly changed.

contaminated with atmospheric pollutants. An outdoor water tap is best. Most watering can be done through a watering-can, although proprietary equipment is available for hanging-baskets and windowboxes that are just out of reach.

SLUGS AND SNAILS

These are stealth pests and often appear from nowhere, usually at night and especially after a shower of rain. They soon decimate plants in ground-level containers. Standing pots and tubs on bricks helps to prevent their ravages, as well as scattering shingle, gravel and broken eggshells around the container. Slippery tapes are available for encircling pots and tubs – slugs and snails find them difficult, if not impossible, to pass.

Psychological influences

Because container displays can be changed from one year to another, as well as within the same year, patio and courtyard gardening creates vibrancy and the opportunity to continually rethink plans for a garden.

Demand on time

Regular attention is needed, especially throughout summer; plants growing in relatively small amounts of compost need watering at least once a day, and sometimes more. Plants need to have their dead flowers removed, both to keep the display tidy and to encourage the development of further blooms. There is also the need at specific times of the year to plant containers, or to change the display from a winter one to a spring or summer arrangement.

Container gardening

What is container gardening?

Growing plants in a wide range of attractive containers, for placing on patios and terraces as well as in courtyards and other places in gardens, is very popular. Containers range from hanging-baskets and windowboxes, which introduce colour at waist or head height, to others for positioning on the ground or even decorating balconies, edges of flat garage roofs, porches and verandahs. Urns, either on pedestals or positioned on the ground, create distinctive features.

WHY GROW PLANTS IN CONTAINERS?

Advantages

✔ Plants can be positioned where you want them – often near a house so that they can be easily seen. This is ideal for culinary herbs, which can then be seen and readily harvested.

✔ Fragrant plants are readily appreciated.

✔ Changes can be made from one season to another.

✔ Success does not depend on the quality of garden soil, which may be infested by pests and diseases, as well as impoverished.

Disadvantages

✘ Plants need regular watering, especially in summer and where the amount of compost is small.

✘ Regular care and attention is essential for many plants.

✘ Range of plants is limited to those that flourish in small amounts of compost.

Many plants grown in containers create a wealth of fragrances on patios, terraces, courtyards and other areas around a house. Flowers produce rich fragrances, while some conifers have scented foliage which is especially noticeable when rubbed.

POSITIONING AND USING CONTAINERS

Tubs and pots

Groups of tubs and pots create attractive features on patios and terraces, either grouped in small clusters in a sheltered corner or near a patio or kitchen door.

• When in small groups, plants afford each other slight protection from strong, gusty winds, as well as creating a mini-environment that is more congenial and slightly more humid.

• By using pots singly or in small groups, the tops of flights of steps can be made more decorative. Use low plants at the top, and taller ones (perhaps upright conifers with colourful foliage) at the lower end of the steps.

Troughs

Troughs are versatile containers and create captivating displays on their own or with groups of pots.

• Small troughs are ideal for brightening the edges of patios at ground level or, with the aid of metal supports, fitted to the tops of balustrades.

• A decorative trough, with a pot on either side burgeoning with flowers, looks good when placed in front of a window. Leave space between the window and the trough, so that watering and maintenance can be carried out easily.

POSITIONING AND USING CONTAINERS (CONTINUED)

Mangers and wall-baskets

Mangers and wall-baskets create magnificent display containers against walls. Mangers are 30–72 cm (12–28 in) wide, while wire-framed wall-baskets are 23–50 cm (9–20 in) across.

- Large mangers are excellent for positioning under windows, while small ones are better on walls that are bare and need brightening.
- Use mangers and wall-baskets in combinations with troughs and plants in pots.
- Position wall-baskets on balcony walls, perhaps on either side of a door. Ensure the door opens freely.

Tubs

Tubs, as well as square and box-like containers, are ideal for shrubs and small trees. They create eye-catching features.

- Use two large containers and plant a half-standard *Laurus nobilis* (Bay) tree in each of them. Position them on either side of an entrance. Full standard trees can be used, but usually they are too dominant and certainly more susceptible to damage from strong wind.
- Round tubs are more informal and are suitable for a dome-topped shrub or small tree.

Miniature water gardens

Position miniature water gardens in slight or variable shade to ensure that the water does not become excessively warm. Also, avoid overhanging trees.

- Position the water feature where it can be easily looked after each day. At the height of summer the water will require regular topping up to compensate for evaporation.
- A grouping of a miniature water garden and an old, shallow, stone sink planted with small rock-garden plants and miniature bulbs never fails to attract attention from passers-by.

Windowboxes

Windowboxes are ideal for creating colour throughout the year. Three distinct arrangements of plants – spring, summer, and winter – in three separate inner boxes are needed, and by rotating them in a decorative outer windowbox it is possible to produce uninterrupted colour from one season to another. Windowboxes bring colour to both sash and casement windows; for sash windows, place on a strong sill, while for casement types on brackets slightly below the sill.

Herb pots and planters

Herb planters are ideal for positioning on patios and near kitchen doors. Herbs can also be grown in pots, and these are best displayed in small clusters or in combination with the herb planter.

- Herb planters, with their informal appearance, are ideal for rustic patios perhaps surfaced with old stone slabs and with gaps left between them for small plants such as Thyme.
- Try positioning a herb planter on a paving slab at the end of a flower border.

Hanging-baskets

Hanging-baskets are versatile and can be used in many exciting and colourful ways. They need to be hung either from a sturdy hook or from a bracket attached to a wall. Here are a few display situations to consider.

- Use two baskets on either side of a window. Position them so that the edges of the display slightly intrude on the window frame.
- Suspend a few hanging-baskets along the edge of a verandah.
- The ends of car-ports benefit from colour, but ensure that you will not bump into the baskets.
- Dull and bland courtyard walls are soon brightened by the addition of a hanging-basket.

Patios and decking areas

What are the options?

For play and leisure areas other than a lawn (see page 10), patios and decking are ideal. Laying a patio takes longer than building decking, which can have a more immediate impact and, apart from the need for supporting bricks or concrete footings, does not involve mixing vast amounts of concrete. Decking is also superb where the soil is uneven and radically sloped. There is a wide choice of patio materials for creating an attractive, yet functional, all-weather surface.

PATIO SHAPE, STYLE AND PLACEMENT

Gone are the days when the best you could hope for in patio comfort was eight grey concrete slabs and two old armchairs; now you can have a patio in just about any shape, colour and style that takes your fancy. A patio is now considered to be more an extension of the house than just a level area in the garden. Just as you want to make the best of the various rooms in your house, now you can shape and decorate the patio to suit your desires and needs.

A basic rectangular patio is a good low-cost option for a small garden.

Geometric combinations – circles and rectangles are wonderfully dynamic – can be used to create separate patio 'rooms', with some areas being set at different levels to increase the visual interest.

PATIO OPTIONS

↗ *An existing patio extended with gravel, cobblestones and stepping stones.*

↗ *This patio has been created using a mixture of old bricks, stone and tiles.*

↗ *An unusual patio made from worn slate inside a hexagonal border.*

← *If you want something a bit different, the strong shape of this circle looks great set within lawn and plants.*

← *For a decorative patio, you could try mixing plain setts and cobblestones in a pretty pattern.*

DECKING OPTIONS

Increasingly, decking forms a major part of leisure areas. A range of decking styles – from ground-level to raised and split-level – are featured here. Raised decking, constructed of a strong and durable wooden framework and supported by wooden or concrete posts cemented into the ground, is a good option for sloping ground or where you have to work over drains and old foundations. Alternatively, decking tiles can be laid on sharp sand at ground level, but they often have a limited life.

↗ *Pattern of colourful decking tiles.*

↗ *Split-level decking is ideal on slopes.*

↗ *Decking built around an existing tree.*

↗ *Raised decking creates a distinctive feature.*

ELEVATED AND ATTACHED

Most decking is elevated, attached to a house and especially useful where ground falls away dramatically from the house. Elevated decking in such a position needs built-in steps; if they are constructed on the side, this often avoids the cost of long and expensive steps positioned at the front of the decking, where the height difference is greatest.

BALUSTRADES

These are essential on raised decking, especially where the height difference from the ground to the decking is great. Balustrades can be formed of wood or ornamental wrought iron. Ensure that they are strong, with no sharp edges that can harm children.

ADVANTAGES OF DECKING

Raised decking is more than an elevated patio, attached to a house or as a free-standing feature within a garden. It can be built at the side of a pond, or even partly over it, as well as over inhospitable ground that needs labour-intensive and expensive reclamation.

ECONOMY DECKING

Decking, especially when formed of multilevel designs, is expensive and time-consuming to construct. An alternative way is to use breeze blocks that are half-buried in the ground and with their surfaces at a uniform height. The breeze blocks can be cemented into the ground. Position 3 m (10 ft) long and 10 cm (4 in) square fencing posts on top, secure them to the breeze blocks and nail pressure-treated gravel boards on top, with spaces between them.

MATERIALS

Use Western Red Cedar or wood that has been pressure-treated with a wood preservative. Brick, concrete or wood (or a combination of them) is essential for supporting piers, while the decking is secured to the joist by galvanized or brass screws with their heads countersunk into the wood. Leave a 6–12 mm (¼–½ in) gap between the planks so that water rapidly drains from the decking's surface.

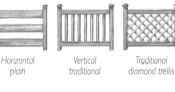

Angled 45° to the joists	*Angle-cut zigzag*	*Square-cut herringbone*
Checkerboard parquet	*At right angles to joists*	*Diamond frame*

Laying the boards in different patterns will add visual interest to the deck.

Horizontal plain	*Vertical traditional*	*Traditional diamond trellis*
Modern square trellis	*Modern 'Chinese' trellis*	*1930s sunburst*

The design of the balustrade can also transform the appearance of a deck.

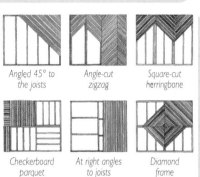

Simple three-tread steps are good for a low deck and are easy to fix.

Open-plan steps with a fancy fretted balustrade are more complicated, but can look stunning.

TREE SEAT

Where a large, long-trunked, decorative tree is within the proposed area of decking, integrate it into the design; lay decking planks around it and encircle it with a wooden seat.

Winter Maintenance

Where decking is in shade and water rests on the surface, it is inevitable that algae will cover the wood and make it unsightly as well as slippery. Use an algicide to remove it.

Family gardens

What is a family garden?

By its nature and timing, a family garden is often the first recreational area that a household creates, and although the demands upon it change it is always a functioning outdoor environment, a summer extension of home living. Young children, however, seldom appreciate the aesthetic qualities of a garden, only viewing its practicality, and when kicking a football over a lawn are seldom bothered by worn-out grass. However, families evolve and needs change.

MULTI-SKILLED QUALITIES

Footballs are, perhaps, the most popular pieces of sports equipment and apart from being kicked can encourage and hone many skills in youngsters. However, avoid repeatedly bouncing balls near a neighbour's garden as it may cause annoyance.

COMPROMISE DESIGNS

With planning, a garden can be all things to each family member. But this is not easy and usually the garden becomes a compromise of play areas for children and ornamental and relaxing places for adults. The proportion of a garden divided between these features changes throughout a family's development and can be made easier by:
- Initially creating a long-term leisure area around your house.
- Growing vegetables and fruit at the far end of a garden where, over the years, the soil can be regularly improved by the addition of well-decomposed garden compost and manure.
- Initially dividing the middle section into a toddlers area (to be used later for sports) and ornamental features. In later years, the entire middle section can be devoted to ornamental features.

Memorable trees

There are many memories and events in a family's life that can be recaptured by planting an ornamental tree or shrub. Marriages and births are times for rejoicing and fragrance is especially valuable as a memory jogger. Lilac was earlier widely used in wedding bouquets and a white-flowered variety grown as a half-standard and planted as a central theme in a lawn never fails to re-conjure memories.

PLAY AREAS FOR CHILDREN

Keeping toddlers busy

Toddlers need a safe, preferably flat, area in which to play and explore life. Together with tricycles, scooters and bicycles they are not respecters of choice plants surrounding the area. Additionally, ensure that nearby plants are children-friendly and do not have thorns. Shallow water troughs are ideal in summer; they can also be drained and used as sandpits.

Damage limitation designs

Covered picnic area

Screen

Bark chippings

Climbing log

Rather than giving all of a garden over to boisterous youngsters, it is better to limit them to an area of their own, but one which (for safety reasons) can be seen from a house window. Children abound with imagination and this needs to be encouraged and channelled into further activities, either practical or ones that need theoretical research.

Simple features, such as old trees and logs, become major play features; a bark chipping base helps to protect youngsters.

Small gardens

Small gardens, when compared with a similarly sized area within a large garden, encourage and need greater gardening involvement, especially when creating a well-admired display throughout the year. Parts of a large garden often escape rigorous and detailed assessment from visitors and there is always the explanation of it being too large. Within a small garden, you must be prepared for continuous and detailed involvement.

Will it need less attention?

OPPORTUNITIES AND CONSTRAINTS

Constructing a lightly shaded patio, perhaps alongside raised beds and with a small pond generating summer interest, is idyllic – and just one opportunity in a small garden. Additionally, there are plants in containers, many colourful and fragrant and acting as reminders of warmer climates. Therefore, be prepared to spend more money than for an equivalent area in a larger garden. Small is beautiful, but sometimes more expensive.

WHAT'S POSSIBLE?

Clearly, garden features that demand unrestricted space are not possible in a small or even moderately sized garden, but many others can be considered. Here are examples of designs for front and rear gardens, and the features that can be included in them.

↗ *Plants in containers introduce colour and a range of shapes to a small front garden.*

← *Even within a small garden, a surprisingly wide range of features can be included. Here, the pergola acts as a focal point, with an informal path leading to a dainty arch.*

LAWN OR PATIO?

In many gardens, both a lawn and a patio are practical features. A lawn unites a garden and creates an attractive foil for borders and beds, whereas a patio is much needed as a year-round, all-weather surface, as well as for summer relaxation. Therefore, in a small garden it is a lawn that is least necessary. This also saves on the storage of lawn tools and mowers – and, perhaps, petrol.

CREATING SPACE

Even in a small garden it is possible to create an impression of space. Aim to have an open area in the centre of the garden, surrounded by plants or features that do not obstruct views to the full extent of the garden. Ponds encourage a perception of space, with the benefit of reflected light creating an impression of an even larger area.

CREATING SURPRISE

There is a delicate balance in a small garden between creating space and ensuring surprise. Both are essential and the surprise element is best near to the edges of the garden, where perhaps a small leaf-clad arch or screen can be combined with perimeter fencing or a wall. A free-standing trellis, dressed with leafy or flowering climbers, is another way to create surprise.

CREATING PRIVACY

Quiet areas are essential in gardens and privacy has healing and supportive properties. Contemplative areas encourage relaxation; leafy vertical and overhead screens ensure seclusion, especially in summer and when clothed with leaves. *Humulus lupulus* 'Aureus' (Yellow-leaved Hop) is ideal for summer privacy; for all-year screening large-leaved variegated Ivies are better.

Need a shed?

In a large garden, a shed is essential as a place for keeping tools, pots and composts, as well as other equipment. In a small garden, consider a combined summerhouse and shed, or even just rely on a garage, if you have one. Ensure that the shed is accessible throughout the year from an all-weather path.

Large gardens

Time and expense are the main problems with planning, constructing and looking after a large garden. Yet there are ways to make life easier, taking advantage of the extra space while creating privacy and seclusion. When confronting a new and large garden, rather than initially tackling the entire area, first create a manageable area around the house, perhaps constructing a patio or area of decking. Always tackle the garden in manageable parts.

FIRST THINGS FIRST

A firm, all-weather surface around a house is the first consideration, whether as a terrace or patio, or even decking if the area is severely sloped, the ground full of large rocks or it has a wealth of drain covers that makes a paved area difficult to construct. Once this is in place, a free-standing trellis helps to separate this 'tamed' area from the rest of the garden.

CHECKING THE DRAINAGE

If the soil remains continually wet, check that the drainage is all right (see page 24). Good drainage is essential and it is best to install land drains before any major planting is attempted, such as ornamental trees and shrubs (see pages 56 and 57) and tree and soft fruits (see pages 66 to 69).

LONG-GRASS AREAS

Where a garden is extra large and in the long-term could become a time and work problem for your family, consider creating a wildlife area, with wide grass paths through and around it. If established trees (either orchard or ornamental types) are present, mow the grass under them to create a relaxed area with rustic seats and tables (see opposite page). A further choice is a rustic summer house at the end of the garden (see opposite page).

WILD-FLOWER MEADOWS

If you are fortunate and have inherited a meadow-like area that has not been cultivated for several generations, it may be rich in native plants, as well as insects and small animals. They therefore need to be protected from disturbance.

LARGE GARDEN PLANS

A formal landscape design

Fountain in raised pond at centre of garden

Low *Buxus sempervirens* (Box) hedges define centre side borders

Evergreen hedges with niche for clipped *Laurus nobilis* (Bay) in container

Brick path

Neatly trimmed lawns

Floribunda roses

↑ Formal gardens have a clinical symmetry that keeps the mind alert. Such gardens need regular attention to keep them tidy.

Creating a wildlife water garden

↑ Wildlife water areas encourage the presence of a wide range of native creatures, including birds, insects, small animals and amphibians.

MORE IDEAS FOR LARGE GARDENS

Rock and water garden

↗ Merging a rock garden with a water garden creates an attractive feature, especially during spring and summer. Pumps can be used to re-cycle the water.

Orchard Gardens

➜ Mowed grass around old orchard trees become oases of peace and tranquillity. Rustic garden furniture completes the scene.

Focal points

➜ Tall and dominant yellow foliaged conifers create focal points throughout the year. Plant colour-contrasting heathers around them.

Bamboo retreats

➜ A screen of bamboos around a garden seat creates a private area, and the rustling of the leaves introduces a constantly refreshed sound.

Coloured bark

➜ A group of Silver Birches are superb in spring, when low rays from the sun glance off the bark. An under planting of crocuses introduces further spring colour.

Summer houses

➜ Rustic summer houses, perhaps tucked away at the end of a garden, are ideal contemplative places when inspiration is needed. They are also areas for reflection.

Winter colour

↗ Many trees and shrubs are invaluable for introducing colour during the winter season. Choose colour- and shape-contrasting plants.

Autumn colour

↗ In autumn, the leaves of many shrubs and trees become attractively coloured. Additionally, many have beautiful spring and summer flowers.

Hardy annuals

Hardy annuals complete their life cycle in one season. They are sown outdoors in spring and early summer in the positions in which they will grow and produce flowers and seeds. With the onset of frosts and cold weather in autumn, these soft-natured plants soon die. You need to pull up these plants, and place them on a compost heap so that they decay and are converted into a material that you can dig into the soil or use as a mulch.

The Californian Poppy (Eschscholzia californica), *a popular hardy annual, creates a wealth of colour from early to late summer.*

Advantages of hardy annuals

Hardy annuals are versatile plants and can be used in several ways. These include:

• In beds and borders totally dedicated to them.

• In displays that can be changed each year.

• As fillers in herbaceous borders and mixed borders.

• As inexpensive and fast-growing fillers in rock gardens, while young plants are becoming established.

• To create a varied range of flowers for use in flower arrangements to decorate rooms.

• To produce a wide range of fragrances.

• A few when dried are 'everlasting', and can be used to create displays throughout winter.

Season of colour

Hardy annuals flower throughout summer, until the frosts of autumn kill the plants. When their display is over, pull the plants up and place them on a compost heap. This can later be used as a mulch or for digging into the soil.

WHEN TO SOW HARDY ANNUALS

It is a waste of time and seeds to sow hardy annuals too early in the year, when the soil is still wet and cold. In such conditions, seeds will not germinate and may even start to decay if the soil is exceptionally wet and cold. Sowing occurs mainly in mid- and late spring, although in cold areas early summer is better.

PREPARING THE SOIL

In late autumn or winter, dig the soil, remove roots of perennial weeds, such as docks, thistles and bindweed, and mix in bulky organic materials such as well-decomposed farmyard manure or garden compost.

• Remember that beds on sunny slopes can be sown earlier than those that are shady, while hollows remain cold and inhospitable for several weeks longer than raised areas. Also, sandy soils are workable earlier than heavy clay types.

• Should the soil not be ready for sowing seeds, do not walk on it as this unevenly consolidates the surface and damages its structure. Also, depressions left by feet, especially on clay soil, may become full of water.

THINNING SEEDLINGS

When seedlings are large enough to handle, carefully thin them without unduly disturbing the soil and loosening the roots of the remaining seedlings. Put the seedlings that are removed on the compost heap; do not leave them on the soil's surface to decay, as they then encourage the presence of pests and diseases. Then, lightly but thoroughly water the soil's surface.

SUPPORTING HARDY ANNUALS

After thinning seedlings, insert twiggy sticks around them. Cut off the tops of twiggy sticks to slightly less than the expected heights of the plants.

SOWING HARDY ANNUALS

When the surface of the soil is friable and dry enough to be walked on, sowing can begin. Some gardeners sow hardy annuals by just scattering seeds on the surface and lightly raking them into the soil. However, a better way is to sow them in shallow drills, thereby enabling seedlings to be easily identified and thinned out; this ensures that they all have equal amounts of space in which to develop. It also makes weed removal easier. Therefore, when you are sowing hardy annuals:

- Use an iron rake to initially level the surface. Then, uniformly consolidate the soil by systematically shuffling sideways over the entire area with your feet. Although time-consuming, this task is essential.
- Again use an iron rake to level the surface and to remove foot prints.
- Use a pointed stick – or a line of dry, sharp sand – to mark out the individual areas where different groups of seeds will be sown. Make them of differing sizes, with corner areas larger and dominant.

- Within each sowing area, form 12–18 mm (½–¾ in) deep drills about 20 cm (8 in) apart. If possible, make the drills in each sowing area at a different angle to the ones next to it. This helps to prevent the entire bed appearing too regimented. There are two ways to form drills: using a draw hoe guided by a garden line, or with a pointed stick drawn along against the side of a straight piece of wood (this is best for small areas).
- Sow seeds evenly and thinly in the base of each drill.
- Use the back of a metal rake to push and pull friable soil over the seeds. Then, use the top of the rake (with the tines parallel to the soil's surface) to firm soil over the drills. Lastly, and in the same direction as the drills, lightly and shallowly draw the rake over the soil to level the surface.
- Label each sowing area with the name of the annual, together with the date.
- When sowing and labelling is complete, lightly but thoroughly water the entire area without disturbing the seeds.
- To prevent birds scratching the surface, either lay twiggy sticks on the ground, or stretch black cotton over the area (but ensure birds cannot become entangled in it). Remove the sticks or lines of cotton as soon as the seeds germinate (avoid treading on the seedlings or unnecessarily consolidating the soil).

Hardy annuals to try

- *Agrostemma githago* 'Milas' (Corn Cockle)
- *Amaranthus caudatus* (Love-lies-bleeding)
- *Calendula officinalis* (Pot Marigold)
- *Chrysanthemum carinatum* (Annual Chrysanthemum)
- *Clarkia elegans* (Clarkia)
- *Consolida ajacis* (Larkspur)
- *Eschscholzia californica* (Californian Poppy)
- *Gypsophila elegans* (Baby's Breath)
- *Helianthus annuus* (Sunflower)
- *Hibiscus trionum* (Flower-of-an-hour)
- *Iberis umbellata* (Candytuft)
- *Lavatera trimestris* (Annual Mallow)
- *Limnanthus douglasii* (Poached Egg Plant)
- *Linaria maroccana* (Toadflax)
- *Linum grandiflorum* 'Rubrum' (Scarlet Flax)
- *Linum usitatissimum* (Common Flax)
- *Lobularia maritima* (Sweet Alyssum)
- *Lychnis viscaria* (Annual Campion)
- *Malcolmia maritima* (Virginia Stock)
- *Matthiola bicornis* (Night-scented Stock)
- *Nigella damascena* (Love-in-a-mist)
- *Papaver rhoeas* (Field Poppy)
- *Papaver somniferum* (Opium Poppy)
- *Reseda odorata* (Mignonette)
- *Scabiosa atropurpurea* (Sweet Scabious)

For hardy annuals for cutting for room decoration

- *Amaranthus caudatus* (Love-lies-bleeding)
- *Gypsophila elegans* (Baby's Breath)
- *Nigella damascena* (Love-in-a-mist)
- *Reseda odorata* (Mignonette)
- *Scabiosa atropurpurea* (Sweet Scabious)

Four fragrant hardy annuals

- *Limnanthus douglasii* (Poached Egg Plant)
- *Matthiola bicornis* (Night-scented Stock)
- *Reseda odorata* (Mignonette)
- *Scabiosa atropurpurea* (Sweet Scabious)

Spring-flowering bedding plants

What are spring-flowering bedding plants?

These include hardy biennials and spring-flowering bulbs, such as tulips. Biennials are sown in spring and early summer for flowering during the following year; they are usually then discarded. Many biennials, however, will continue growing if you leave them. Spring-flowering bulbs are planted in late summer or early autumn and flower during the following spring. Tulips are the most popular spring-flowering bedding bulbs and can be mixed with biennials.

Wallflowers never fail to create colour and reliable displays in spring and early summer. Plant in combination with tulips.

Advantages of biennials

These are resilient and hardy plants that survive outdoors throughout winter and create magnificent displays in spring and early summer. They can be bought from nurseries and garden centres, or raised yourself from seeds (see opposite page).

Season of colour

Most flower during spring and early summer, although some continue throughout most of summer (see below).

Advantages of tulips

Bulbs are nature's powerhouses of stored energy and seldom fail to produce a superb display. Tulips are planted in late summer or early autumn, in holes 3–4 times their own depth, and in late spring and early summer produce magnificent flowers in a wide range of colours.

RAISING BIENNIALS

A small seed-bed area in which seeds can be sown is essential; the soil needs to be well-drained yet moisture-retentive, with a friable surface for easy seed sowing. Here is the way to produce these conditions:

- In late autumn or early winter, dig a piece of well-drained ground in a warm, lightly shaded and sheltered position. Remove all perennial weeds.
- Leave the area alone during winter, and in late spring or early summer prepare the soil. First, rake the area level, then systematically shuffle sideways over it to uniformly consolidate the soil. Then, use a rake to level the surface and to create an even tilth into which seeds can be sown.
- Insert 30 cm (1 ft) long sticks, 23 cm (9 in) apart, along opposite sides of the seedbed. Then, stretch a garden line between a pair of them and use a draw hoe to take out a drill 12–18 mm (30–45 in) deep. Ensure that the base of the drill has a uniform depth.
- Sow seeds evenly and thinly in the base, taking care not to let them fall in clusters. Do not sow seeds directly from the packet; rather, tip a few seeds in one hand and allow them to pass out between your thumb, index finger and middle finger into the drill. Do not feel obliged to

sow a complete packet of seeds in a single drill; this usually produces masses of seedlings that become congested, etiolated and susceptible to diseases.

- Cover the seeds by using the back of a metal rake to push and pull friable soil over them, but taking care not to disturb them. Then, use the flat head of the rake to firm the soil; it is essential that the soil is in close contact with the seeds, as this encourages even germination. If the surface of the soil over the row is uneven, shallowly use the rake to level the soil, but without disturbing the seeds.
- Mark the ends of the row with the name of the seeds and the date.
- If the soil is very dry, lightly but thoroughly water the entire seed bed. Do not just dampen the soil's surface, as this will encourage roots to form near the surface and not to establish themselves deeper in the soil.

GERMINATING AND THINNING

- Keep the seed bed free from weeds, both between the rows and the seedlings, and during dry weather lightly but thoroughly water the soil – do not just dampen the surface soil, as this will do more harm than good.
- When the seedlings are large enough to handle, either thin them out or transplant to a nursery bed; thinning them is the easier method, however.
- If seeds have been sown thinly, the ensuing plants are relatively spaced out. Small biennials, such as *Bellis perennis* (Double Daisy) are thinned 7.5–10 cm (3–4 in) apart, whereas larger and taller ones, like *Erysimum cheiri* (Wallflower), are left 13–15 cm (5–6 in) apart.
- Where seeds have been sown close together, use a garden fork to lift young plants as soon as they can be handled, and replant them into a nursery bed, spacing them 15–23 cm (6–9 in) apart in rows 30 cm (1 ft) apart. A few days before lifting plants for replanting, water both the seed bed and the nursery bed into which they will be planted. Young plants which are put into dry soil seldom succeed, even if you water them generously afterwards.

PLANTING BIENNIALS AND TULIPS

Tulips and wallflowers, as well as *Bellis perennis* (Double Daisy), form superb features in spring and early summer.

- Plant biennials into gardens in late summer or early autumn, especially if you are planting them into beds with bulbs such as tulips.
- Prepare the bed by removing all vegetation and digging it to remove perennial weeds and to improve drainage and aeration. Rake and lightly firm the soil's surface.
- Position the tulip bulbs on the soil's surface, spacing them 15–23 cm (6–9 in) apart; interplant them with *Erysimum cheiri* (Wallflower) about 25 cm (10 in) apart, and Double Daisies (*Bellis perennis*) 13 cm (5 in) apart. Then plant the bulbs so they are covered with 2–3 times their own depth of soil.

CLASSIC SPRING COMBINATIONS

Tulips are popular for growing with biennials to create attractive shape and colour contrasts in spring. Here are a few to consider:

- Tulips are traditional companions for Wallflowers and Forget-me-knots. Cottage-type Tulips, with their large, egg-shaped heads, stand proudly above these underplantings and create a magnificent display.
- Tulips blend with a carpet planting of Double Daisies. For harmonies in blue, plant blue-flowered Parrot-type Tulips with the Forget-me-nots.
- Choose dark red Darwin-type Tulips and combine them with white Pansies.
- Plant the single-early Tulip 'Kelzerskoon' (with yellow and red flowers) with an underplanting of a yellow viola.

THE NATURE OF BIENNIALS

Biennials are raised from seed sown during one year for flowering in the following one. However, not everything with biennials is straightforward and although some, such as Foxgloves and Forget-me-knots, are natural biennials, others, like Hollyhocks, Daisies and Wallflowers, are hardy perennials usually grown as biennials.

Holy thoughts

The popular Hollyhock is claimed to have been first introduced into Britain from Palestine by returning Crusaders about 800 years ago, when it was called 'Holy-hoc'. Hoc was the Anglo-Saxon word for a mallow.

Hardy biennials to consider

Although many biennials flower in spring and early summer, others produce their display later. Part of this disparity is that many of them are hardy perennials grown as biennials. Here are the flowering times of the most popular plants grown as biennials. Not all of them are suitable for spring-flowering bedding plant displays.

- *Alcea rosea* (Hollyhock): mid-summer to early autumn.
- *Bellis perennis* (Common Daisy): mid-spring to mid-autumn.
- *Campanula medium* (Canterbury Bell): early and mid-summer.
- *Dianthus barbatus* (Sweet William): early and mid-summer.
- *Digitalis purpurea* (Foxglove): early to late summer.
- *Erysimum* x *allionii* (Siberian Wallflower): late spring to mid-summer.
- *Erysimum cheiri* (Wallflower): mid-spring to early summer.
- *Myosotis alpestris* (Forget-me-not): late spring to early summer.

Two fragrant biennials

- *Dianthus barbatus* (Sweet William)
- *Erysimum cheiri* (Wallflower)

Summer-flowering bedding plants

These are half-hardy annuals that are sown in seed-trays (flats) in gentle warmth in greenhouses in late winter and early spring. After germination, the seedlings are transferred to wider spacings in further seed-trays (flats). Later, the plants need to be acclimatized to outdoor conditions before being planted into beds and borders. These plants are tender and are easily damaged by late spring frosts. They are also planted in containers.

Advantages of summer-flowering bedding plants

- Wide range of types, in many colours and heights. Most have a bushy habit, although some trail and are ideal for planting in hanging-baskets and along the sides of windowboxes.
- Displays can be altered each year.
- When displays finish, spring-flowering plants, including biennials and bulbs (see pages 48–49), can be put in their place to create colour in the spring.

Season of colour

These plants flower from late spring and early summer to the plant-killing frosts of autumn.

GLASS AND NEWSPAPER

After sowing, the seed-tray (flat) needs to be covered to prevent the surface of the compost drying. There are a couple of ways of doing this:

- Traditionally, a piece of glass was put over the seed-tray (flat). However, condensation forms on the underside and needs to be wiped clear every morning. The glass is then inverted, so that the dry side is facing the compost. To create a dark environment (needed by most seeds to aid germination), place a sheet of newspaper on top. This must be removed as soon as seeds germinate.
- More recently, transparent dome covers that fit seed-trays (flats) have been used and these are ideal where children might approach the seedlings and become cut by glass. They can be washed after use and stored for the following year.

RAISING SUMMER-FLOWERING BEDDING PLANTS

When raising summer-flowering bedding plants, greenhouses provide assured warmth in which seeds can germinate and young seedlings grow healthily.

1 *Fill a seed-tray (flat) with fresh seed compost and use your fingers to firm it, especially around the edges. Then, refill with compost.*

2 *Use a straight piece of wood to level the compost, and a compost presser to firm the surface to about 12 mm (½ in) below the tray's rim.*

3 *Tip a few seeds on a piece of stiff, folded card; tap the end of the card to encourage seeds to fall evenly over the compost's surface, but not near the edges of the tray.*

4 *Use a flat-based horticultural sieve to cover the seeds with compost to 3–4 times their thickness. Alternatively, use a culinary sieve.*

5 *To water the compost, stand the seed-tray (flat) in a flat-based bowl shallowly filled with water. Remove the seed-tray (flat) when the surface of the compost is moist. Allow excess moisture to drain.*

PRICKING OFF SEEDLINGS

1 *After germination, remove the cover. Continue to water the seedlings by standing the seed-tray (flat) in a bowl shallowly filled with water.*

2 *When large enough to handle and be pricked off, water the seedlings without wetting the leaves. Then, use a small fork to place a few seedlings on a piece of damp hessian or newspaper.*

3 *Fill and firm compost in a seed-tray (flat). Use a small dibber to make holes in the compost, keeping the outer row 12 mm (4½ in) from the tray's sides.*

4 *Hold a seedling by one of its leaves and insert the roots into a hole (to the same depth as before). Gently firm compost around them.*

5 *When the seed-tray (flat) is full, gently tap its edges to level loose compost. Gently water the compost from above to settle it around the roots.*

Later ...

After being pricked off, keep the compost lightly moist. When leaves of adjoining seedlings touch each other, plants to be grown as summer-flowering bedding plants can be acclimatized to outdoor conditions by placing them in cold frames; later, plant them outdoors when all risk of frost has passed.

AFTER GERMINATION

After seeds germinate, slowly reduce the temperature and ensure that the young seedlings are given plenty of air. Avoid placing the seedlings in strong and direct sunlight. As soon as the seedlings are large enough to handle, they must be transferred (pricked off) into further seed-trays (flats), where they can be given more space. Seedlings that are left clustered together in seed-trays (flats) become weak and etiolated, and susceptible to diseases.

PREPARING THE SOIL FOR PLANTING

As soon as spring-flowering plants (biennials and spring-flowering bulbs such as tulips) have finished flowering, dig them up. Place the biennials on a compost heap, while the tulips (complete with dead flowers, stems and bulbs still intact) need to be placed in shallow, slatted boxes and placed in an airy, vermin-proof shed. Leave them there until the foliage and stem detaches from the bulb, which can then be stored until the following autumn. Usually, however, it is better to buy fresh bulbs each autumn.

Half-hardy annual bedding plants

- *Alonsoa warscewiczii* (Mask Flower) – half-hardy perennial usually grown as a half-hardy annual.
- *Amaranthus hypochondriacus* (Prince's Feather) – half-hardy annual.
- *Amaranthus tricolor* (Joseph's Coat) – half-hardy annual.
- *Begonia semperflorens* (Fibrous Begonia/Wax Begonia) – tender perennial usually grown as a half-hardy annual.
- *Cleome spinosa* (Spider Flower) – half-hardy annual.
- *Cosmos bipinnatus* (Mexican Aster) – half-hardy annual.
- *Heliotropium arborescens* (Cherry Pie/Heliotrope) – half-hardy perennial, invariably grown as a half-hardy annual.
- *Lobelia erinus* (Edging Lobelia) – half-hardy perennial invariably grown as a half-hardy annual.
- *Lobularia maritima* (Sweet Alyssum) – earlier and still popularly known as *Alyssum maritimum*, this hardy annual is usually grown as a half-hardy annual.
- *Nicotiana alata* (Tobacco Plant) – half-hardy annual raised for planting into summer-flowering bedding schemes.
- *Petunia x hybrida* (Petunia) – half-hardy perennial invariably grown as a half-hardy annual.
- *Salvia splendens* (Scarlet Salvia) – half-hardy perennial, invariably grown as a half-hardy annual.
- *Tagetes erecta* (Aztec Marigold/African Marigold) – half-hardy annual.
- *Tagetes patula* (French Marigold) – half-hardy annual.
- *Verbena x hybrida* (Verbena) – half-hardy perennial invariably grown as a half-hardy annual.
- *Zinnia elegans* (Youth-and-Old Age) – half-hardy annual.

Herbaceous perennials

Herbaceous perennials have a longer life-span than annuals or biennials, and once planted last for 3–4 years before they become congested; then you need to dig them up and replant young pieces from around the outside of the clump. The inner part is usually discarded. Herbaceous perennials develop fresh shoots from ground level each spring. They bear flowers mainly in summer and with the onset of frosts in autumn the leaves and stems die down.

Advantages of herbaceous perennials

• Plants last for 3–4 years; and even then clumps can be lifted and divided and young pieces replanted.

• Relatively easy to grow – and some do not need to be supported (see below).

• Versatile plants that can be used in gardens in a wide range of ways (see below).

• Many can be cut and used in flower arrangements (see opposite page for a range of plants).

Season of colour

Flowering is mainly during summer, although some create a display in late spring and others into early autumn. Some of these plants also have attractively variegated leaves, and many can be used in indoor flower arrangements.

Twenty self-supporting herbaceous perennials

• *Acanthus* (Bear's Breeches)

• *Achillea* (Yarrow)

• *Anemone x hybrida* (Japanese Anemone)

• *Aconitum* (Monkshood)

• *Alchemilla mollis* (Lady's Mantle)

• *Anaphalis* (Pearl Everlasting)

• *Catananche* (Cupid's Dart)

• *Dicentra* (Bleeding Heart)

• *Echinops* (Globe Thistle)

• *Helenium* (Sneezewort)

• *Limonium* (Sea Lavender)

• *Lupinus* (Lupin)

• *Lychnis chalcedonica* (Jerusalem Cross)

• *Lysimachia* (Loosestrife)

• *Monarda* (Bergamot)

• *Pulmonaria* (Lungwort)

• *Rudbeckia* (Coneflower)

• *Scabiosa* (Scabious)

• *Trollius* (Globe Flower)

• *Verbascum* (Mullein)

USING HERBACEOUS PERENNIALS IN GARDENS

• In earlier years, herbaceous plants were planted in borders totally devoted to them; increasingly, however, they are intermingled with other plants.
• 'Mixed borders' (see pages 54–55) are medleys of different types of plants and, among others, include herbaceous plants, bulbs, tuberous plants such as dahlias, evergreen and deciduous shrubs. There might also be an ornamental tree in the border.
• Having an 'island border' positioned in a large lawn is an excellent way to add colour to a garden. Kidney-shaped beds, 3–3.6 m (10–12 ft) long and 1.8–2.4 m (6–8 ft) wide, are best as this enables plants to be reached without having to tread on the border. If the lawn is large enough, plan for three closely positioned kidney-shaped beds; allow space for 90 cm–1.2 m (3–4 ft) wide paths between them. For ease of maintenance, choose herbaceous plants that do not need to be supported (see right for suitable plants).

RAISING HERBACEOUS PLANTS

Two ways to increase them are by seeds or lifting and dividing them. Sow seeds in drills in a seed bed outdoors in the same manner as biennials (see pages 48).

See the opposite page for how to divide and replant these hardy, resilient, colourful plants.

SUPPORTING HERBACEOUS PERENNIALS

Many herbaceous plants are self-supporting (see above), while others benefit from support. There are three ways:
• Twiggy sticks inserted around young plants so that as stems and leaves develop they hide the twigs.
• Stakes knocked into soil around plants, with garden string tied around them to encapsulate the plant. This is an excellent way to support dahlias.
• Proprietary metal supports, usually in two pieces and each with a curved top to form a circle around a plant.

Ten herbaceous perennials to raise from seeds

- *Acanthus mollis* (Bear's Breeches)
- *Acanthus spinosus* (Bear's Breeches)
- *Achillea* (Yarrow)
- *Campanula* (some species)
- *Centaurea* (some species)
- *Dictamnus albus* (Burning Bush)
- *Echinacea purpurea* (Purple Cone Flower)
- *Leucanthemum maximum* (Shasta Daisy)
- *Lupinus polyphyllus* (but not named varieties)
- *Sisyrinchium*

DIVISION

Congested clumps can be lifted and divided at any time between early autumn and mid-spring, whenever the weather and soil are suitable. This usually means autumn in areas where the weather is mild, but spring is better in cold regions.

1 *Use sharp secateurs to cut away old stems still remaining on the clump, and a garden fork to lift the clump from underneath. Then, insert two garden forks, back to back, into the clump and draw the handles together to lever it apart.*

2 *Use your hands to further separate the clump. However, avoid producing very small pieces. Use a hand trowel to plant individual pieces into a bed or border. Firm the soil and water the entire area.*

Ten herbaceous perennials to increase by division

- *Achillea* (Yarrow)
- *Anaphalis* (Pearl Everlasting)
- *Astrantia* (Masterwort)
- *Coreopsis* (Tickseed)
- *Filipendula* (Dropwort)
- *Lysimachia* (Loosestrife)
- *Lythrum* (Purple Loosestrife)
- *Monarda* (Bergamot)
- *Rudbeckia* (Coneflower)
- *Solidago* (Golden Rod)

Five scented herbaceous perennials

- *Dictamnus albus* (Burning Bush)
- *Filipendula ulmaria* (Meadowsweet)
- *Monarda didyma* (Bergamot)
- *Nepeta x faassenii* (Catmint)
- *Saponaria officinalis* (Common Soapwort)

Ten herbaceous perennials for flower arrangements

- *Achillea* (Fern-leaf Yarrow)
- *Alchemilla* (Lady's Mantle)
- *Dicentra spectabilis* (Bleeding Heart)
- *Gypsophila paniculata* (Baby's Breath)
- *Helenium autumnale* (Sneezewort)
- *Limonium latifolium* (Sea Lavender)
- *Lychnis chalcedonica* (Jerusalem Cross)
- *Scabiosa caucasica* (Scabious)
- *Solidago* (Golden Rod)
- *Thalictrum dipterocarpum* (Meadow Rue)

Flowers and seed heads for drying for winter decoration

- *Acanthus*
- *Achillea*
- *Anaphalis*
- *Echinops*
- *Eryngium*
- *Gypsophila*
- *Limonium*
- *Onopordum*
- *Physalis*

Mixed borders

What are mixed borders?

Mixed borders are a medley of many different plants, including herbaceous perennials, biennials, shrubs and, perhaps, an ornamental tree. They are often also planted with bulbs and tubers, with hardy annuals and summer-flowering bedding plants (half-hardy annuals) added to fill gaps, especially when the border is new and other plants are not fully established. Most flower borders in gardens are of this type and they create colour from spring to autumn.

MIXED-BORDER OCCUPANTS

- **Hardy annuals:** see pages 46–47
- **Summer-flowering bedding plants:** see pages 50–51
- **Biennials:** see pages 48–49
- **Herbaceous perennials:** see pages 52–53
- **Shrubs and trees:** see pages 56–57
- **Bulbs:** botanically, they are underground storage organs, with a bud-like structure and formed of fleshy scales attached to a flattened base called a basal plate. Onions, daffodils and tulips are examples of bulbs. They invariably produce an eye-catching display. Some bulbs are spring-flowering; others bloom during summer.
- **Corms:** these have a similar energy-storing function to bulbs, but with a different structure. They are formed of a laterally thickened stem base, usually covered with a papery skin. Each year, a new corm forms at the top of the old one. Crocuses and gladioli are examples of corms. Many corms, such as some species of crocuses, flower in spring (others in autumn), while gladioli create their display in summer, and a few into early autumn.
- **Tubers:** botanically, a tuber is a swollen, thickened and often fleshy stem or root. For example, some tubers are swollen roots (dahlias), while others are swollen stems (potatoes). They are all storage organs that perpetuate plants from one season to another. Dahlias are popular in mixed borders, where they flower mainly during late summer and into early autumn. Incidentally, these are usually known as 'border' dahlias to distinguish them from bedding dahlias, which are raised as annuals from seeds.

Advantages of mixed borders

- A wide range of different types of plants can be grown in the same border.
- Ideal for small gardens as they contain a range of different types of plants, from perennials to bulbs and annuals.
- Filler plants (biennials and summer-flowering bedding plants) can be varied each year.

Season of colour

Spring-flowering bulbs and biennials usually create the first colour of the year in mixed borders, with the display continued throughout summer and into autumn by herbaceous perennials, shrubs, summer-flowering bulbs and tuberous-rooted plants such as dahlias. Where possible, have a few winter-flowering shrubs (see pages 56–57 for suitable types).

- **Rhizomes:** these are another form of energy-storage organ; they grow horizontally and, while some are totally under-ground, others are partly buried. They can be either slender or fleshy and thick. For example, some irises, such as *Iris germanica* (Flag Iris), have thick and fleshy rhizomes which are partly buried, while *Convallaria majalis* (Lily-of-the-valley), has slender and spreading rhizomes, mostly shallowly buried beneath the soil's surface.

This border is packed with summer colour. It is illustrated again on the opposite page during spring, autumn and winter, when other plants are in flower.

DIVIDING DAHLIA TUBERS

In autumn, about a week after their foliage has been blackened by frost, use a garden fork to lift tubers from borders where they have been growing. Cut stems to 15 cm (6 in) high and position upside down for a couple of weeks in an airy shed. Then place in boxes of slightly damp peat.

 *In early to mid-spring, use a sharp knife to divide clumps of tubers; each new plant must contain a stem (which contains growth buds).*

 *Alternatively, where there are only a few stems, cut these in half vertically. Each part of the stem must have at least one healthy growth bud.*

Dust cut surfaces with a fungicide, then plant individual pieces directly into a border, in holes 15 cm (6 in) deep. Before you plant, insert a cane to mark the position of the tuber.

Spring is full of vitality and new growth, with many early-flowering plants revealing colour.

Autumn is often considered to be an afterthought, but in this border variegated shrubs continue the colour.

Winter reveals winter-flowering Pansies, berried shrubs and those plants with a display of variegated leaves.

DIVIDING RHIZOMATOUS IRISES

Lifting and dividing rhizomes of *Iris germanica* (Flag Iris) as soon as its flowers fade will ensure that flower quality does not diminish. Alternatively, lift and divide the rhizomes in late summer.

Carefully dig up the entire plant and use a sharp knife to divide clumps, selecting young pieces from around the outside. Discard old, central parts.

 Each piece must have one or two fans of leaves. Trim off the top third of the foliage.

Replant the young plants, either in a nursery bed or in a border, to the same depth as before.

Bulbs

Bulbils develop around the parent bulbs. After the plant has flowered and when the foliage has died down naturally, lift the bulbs and carefully remove the bulbils. In late summer or early autumn, large bulbils can be replanted.

Small bulbils take about two seasons before they are large enough to produce flowers. In autumn, form a flat-based drill, 5–7.5 cm (2–3 in) deep, with sharp sand in its base. Space the bulbils their own width apart and cover them with friable soil. After two years, lift and plant them in their flowering positions.

Corms

Towards autumn, old corms shrivel, leaving a new one that will flower during the following year. Additionally, cormlets cluster around its base. In autumn, carefully fork up plants and cut each stem 12 mm (½ in) above the corm. Discard the old, shrivelled corm and in winter store the new one in a dry, vermin-proof shed.

Remove the cormlets; place in a dry shed during winter. In early spring, form a drill 5 cm (2 in) deep and line it with sharp sand; space the cormlets their own width apart and cover with friable soil. Lift them in autumn and store in winter. Repeat this in the following year before they reach flowering size.

Shrub and tree borders

Shrubs and trees introduce permanency to gardens, and whereas shrubs last for ten or more years, trees will be with you for at least 20. Shrubs can be evergreen or deciduous (shed their leaves in autumn and produce a fresh array in spring), and are distinguished by having several stems growing from soil level. Trees can also be evergreen or deciduous, but have just one stem (trunk) that supports a framework of branches with a trunk at least 1.2 m (4 ft) long.

Lavandula angustifolia 'Hidcote' (Lavender) is a hardy, evergreen shrub with purple-blue flowers from mid-summer to early autumn.

WHAT SHRUBS AND TREES CAN DO FOR GARDENS

- Borders entirely created from shrubs and trees. Usually, this way of using them is only suitable for large gardens, although many shrubs are diminutive.
- Create ground cover to suppress the growth of weeds and to stabilize and make steep banks more attractive.
- Form hedges, usually along boundaries, but also within a garden, perhaps to separate a vegetable or fruit plot from an ornamental area. Hardy, evergreen shrubs are usually chosen for boundaries, whereas diminutive evergreen or deciduous types with attractive flowers or leaves are better within a garden.
- Introduce a wide range of fragrances, from almond, cowslip, honey, lemon and lily-of-the-valley to orange blossom. There are many other fragrances and some are created during winter, when they are especially welcome.
- Flowering arches formed by ornamental flowering trees, such as laburnum, are popular. Creating a flowering arch is not quick, but worth the wait. Apple and pear arches are also possible.
- Coloured bark and stems soon gain attention, especially in winter when there is little other colour.
- Flowers are possible throughout the year by choosing a range of shrubs and trees.
- Colourful leaves, many variegated, are produced throughout the year by evergreen shrubs, but during summer only by deciduous types.
- Colourful leaves in autumn are always welcome.
- Clothe walls in spectacular flowers and colourful leaves. Growing a tender climber against a wall gives it protection in winter.
- Topiary, whether formed into cones and spirals or birds and animals, instantly captures attention.

DECIDUOUS OR EVERGREEN TREES AND SHRUBS?

- **Deciduous:** shed their leaves in autumn and create a fresh array in spring.
- **Evergreen:** appear to retain leaves throughout the year, but really are continually shedding old ones and producing new ones.
- **Semi-evergreen:** depending on the winter (if it is mild or severe) some shrubs, such as Privet, may shed some or all of their leaves.

Shrubs and trees in small gardens

In small gardens it is essential to choose a suitable shrub or tree. Here are a few clues to success:

- **Naturally small:** although diminutive, a shrub or tree should have a natural and attractive appearance and not have to be radically pruned in an attempt to keep it small – which invariably does not work.

- **Slow-growing:** avoid shrubs and trees that grow rapidly and soon become too big for their allotted positions. Excessively vigorous plants are a waste of money, as invariably they have to be dug up and removed.

- **Varying interests:** wherever possible, select a shrub or tree that has at least two attractive qualities, perhaps its flowers and leaves.

- **Easy to establish:** rapid and easy establishment are essential, so always buy a healthy plant. Do not buy an inferior one, just because it is cheap.

- **Non-invasive:** check that the shrub or tree is not invasive – meaning that it could soon dominate nearby plants.

DO ALL SHRUBS NEED PRUNING?

Most evergreen shrubs only need pruning to maintain a shapely plant that does not intrude on its neighbours. This is best tackled in mid- or late spring, just when growth is beginning. However, if it is a flowering type, defer pruning until the blooms fade.

Flowering deciduous shrubs need regular pruning to encourage the yearly production of flowers.

- **Early-flowering deciduous shrubs (spring to mid-summer):** prune immediately the flowers fade, cutting back shoots that have flowered.
- **Late-summer-flowering shrubs (mid-summer to autumn):** prune during the following late spring.
- **Winter-flowering shrubs:** these need little pruning. This is performed in spring and, when young, these shrubs need pruning to create an attractive shape. Later, thin out congested stems and those damaged by winter weather.

A medley of shrubs, trees and herbaceous perennials creates borders that remain attractive for many months.

DO TREES NEED PRUNING?

Once established, most trees need little pruning except when young to create a desired shape. Later, misplaced, old and intruding branches may need to be removed; do not prune *Prunus* trees, such as cherries, while they are dormant in winter; wait until they start growing again in spring.

LAYERING A SHRUB

1 *Select a healthy, low-growing, vigorous shoot that is up to two years old. Form a shallow trench that slopes to 7.5–15 cm (3–6 in) deep at its lowest point, 23–45 cm (9–18 in) from the shoot's tip. Lower the shoot into the depression and bend its tip upright. Wound the stem, either by making a tongued cut at the point of the bend or by cutting halfway around the stem and removing the bark.*

2 *Use a piece of bent wire or a wooden peg to hold the stem in the ground. Firm soil over the stem, so that its surface is level. Insert a bamboo cane and tie the shoot to it, to hold it secure and upright.*

3 *When new growth appears on the layered shoot, remove the soil, sever the shoot from the parent and plant into a nursery bed or directly into a border.*

Twenty shrubs, trees and climbers that can be layered

This is an easy way to increase plants, although it takes up to a year for roots to form on the layered part.

- *Amelanchier* (June Berry/Snowy Mespilus)
- *Azalea* • *Chaenomeles* (Japanese Quince/Cydonia/Japonica) • *Chimonanthus praecox* (Winter Sweet) • *Clematis* • *Cornus alba* (Red-barked Dogwood) • *Cotoneaster* • *Forsythia* (Golden Bells) • *Garrya elliptica* • *Hamamelis* (Witch Hazel) • *Jasminum nudiflorum* (Winter-flowering Jasmine) • *Liriodendron tulipifera* (Tulip Tree) • *Magnolia* • *Parthenocissus* • *Pieris* • *Piptanthus* • *Rhododendron* • *Rhus typhina* (Stag's Horn Sumach) • *Viburnum* • *Wisteria*

Climbing and screening plants

Uses for climbers and wall shrubs range from clothing walls and fences with flowers and colourful leaves to smothering arbours, pergolas and arches in colour. A few climbers can be encouraged to form hedges, clothe old tree stumps and climb into trees. Climbing and rambling roses also have many uses, including clambering over pergolas, covering tripods and pillars and growing into trees. They are often used to cover walls, in either cold or sunny situations.

HOW AND WHERE TO USE CLIMBERS

Climbers are versatile and can be used in many ways. Here are a few ideas on how they can enhance your garden, whether they are clothing walls or, when clambering over a free-standing trellis, creating a screen that blocks off neighbouring gardens or cloaks unsightly features in your own garden, such as dustbins (garbage bins) or fuel-storage tanks.

Clothing walls

↘ Both flowering and coloured-leaved climbers will clothe walls. Some climbers are self-supporting, but others need a wall-secured trellis. Large-leaved and variegated ivies (right) always create an attractive screen.

Pergolas

↘ Pergolas – whether of a rustic or formal nature – are ideal homes for climbers, especially those such as wisteria with long bunches of fragrant flowers. Some wisterias have white flowers; others blue-purple or mauve.

Arches

↘ Arches – whether dainty and formed of metal hoops, or informal and constructed of rustic poles – create superb homes for flowering and leafy climbers.

Free-standing screens

↘ Square or diamond-shaped trellis panels secured to a series of vertical posts about 1.8 m (6 ft) apart soon create a peep-proof screen when clothed in leaves. These screens help to cloak vegetable and fruit areas.

Into trees

↘ Several vigorous flowering climbers can be planted to clamber into deciduous trees, where they become distinctive features that invariably capture attention.

Tree stumps

↘ After cutting back an old tree, digging out the roots is laborious work. Instead, plant a climber that will clothe the trunk and create an attractive feature.

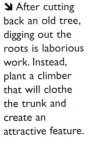

Arbours

↘ Secluded arbours, clothed in fragrant flowers, add distinctive features to gardens. Ensure that a seat or bench for two is fitted into the arbour.

Hedges

↗ A few climbers – whether on their own, in partnership with a shrub or intertwined with a wrought-iron fence – can create an attractive and unusual hedge.

HOW AND WHERE TO USE WALL SHRUBS

Many shrubs can be grown against walls, but with all of them it is essential to have a framework of tiered wires or a trellis to support them. During their early years, many wall shrubs do not appear to need support, but later – and perhaps when they are weighed down by a heavy fall of snow – a supporting framework is essential.

Walls

↑ Many shrubs are ideal for planting against a sunny wall, where tender types gain both wind protection and a warm position. Shady walls can also be clothed.

Screens

↗ In the same way that climbers can create free-standing screens, so too can wall shrubs. In cold areas, however, only frost-hardy ones can be used.

HOW AND WHERE TO USE CLIMBING AND RAMBLING ROSES

Climbing and rambling roses do not create such a dense array of foliage as that produced by many climbers and wall shrubs, but they make up for this with their superb flowers.

There are many ways to use roses in gardens, from covering walls and pergolas to adorning tripods and pillars. Many are ideal for covering tall tree trunks or climbing into trees.

Walls

↗ Roses have long been grown against walls, where they create a feast of summer colour. In general, climbers are better than ramblers against walls.

Tripods and pillars

↙ ↘ Both climbing and rambling roses can be planted to climb tripods and pillars, drenching them in colour. Climbing types are easier to prune than ramblers. Tripods and pillars are ideal for small gardens.

Arches and pergolas

↗ Ramblers, with their pliable stems, are ideal for training over arches and pergolas. However, unlike climbers, ramblers are not normally repeat-flowering.

Tall tree stumps

↘ Old tree trunks, if still sturdy and not at risk from falling over under the weight of rose stems and foliage, can be clothed with foliage and flowers.

Growing into trees

↗ Both climbing and rambling roses can be used, but they need to be vigorous. Once established, roses grown in this way need little attention.

Water plants

What are water plants?

Many different types of plants are known as 'water plants', from those that are totally submerged in water to ones growing in shallow areas at the sides of ponds. Of course there are waterlilies, the epitome of water gardening. There are also plants that like to grow in boggy soil around the edges of informal ponds. Essentially, when selecting these plants, check that they will not become excessively rampant and swamp the pond with stems, flowers and leaves.

Pistia stratiotes *(Water Lettuce) is slightly tender and free-floating.*

Water gently cascading or splashing into a pond creates vibrancy and shimmering reflections on the water's surface.

Eichhornia *(Water Hyacinth) floats on the surface, with orchid-like flowers.*

Nymphaea *'Ellisiana', with rose-red-purple flowers, is a hardy waterlily for planting in water to a depth of 45 cm (18 in).*

Phragmites australis *'Variegatus' is a swamp-loving, spreading perennial.*

POND PLANTS

Floaters
These appear to have no visible means of support, with leaves and stems floating freely on or just below the water's surface, with roots below and usually trailing. Some of these plants have flowers, but most do not.

Marginal plants
These have roots that are submerged and planted in meshed, plastic containers standing on the pond's base or on raised shelves around the edges, but still within the pond. The leaves and flowers are above the water's surface.

Bog-garden plants
Also known as moisture-loving plants, waterside plants and pool-side plants, they are ideal for planting in soil around the edge of an informal pond; the soil needs to be continually moist, but not waterlogged. Leaves, stems and flowers are above the compost's surface.

Oxygenators
Also known as water-weeds and submerged aquatics, plants are totally submerged, with their roots planted in plastic-mesh containers positioned on the pond's base. Occasionally, some of these plants produce flowers.

Waterlilies
Distinctive and popular plants, with roots submerged and planted in plastic-mesh containers positioned on the pond's base. The leaves usually float on the water's surface, with flowers slightly above the surface. The range of varieties is wide, but you need to choose with care to ensure that a vigorous type is not planted in a small pond (see below).

Deep-water aquatics
Also known as deep marginals, their roots are submerged, with leaves and flowers above the water's surface. These plants are best planted in plastic containers with meshed, open sides and positioned on the pond's base.

WATERLILIES FOR ALL PONDS

Before buying a waterlily, always check that it suits the pond's depth and size. Talk to a specialist supplier and take along the dimensions of your pond and its depth. Never plant a waterlily that is too large and vigorous as it soon causes congestion and, eventually, has to be removed.

- **Pygmy waterlilies:** also known as dwarf or miniature waterlilies, they are ideal for small ponds, tubs and deep stone sinks. The depth of water above the plastic-mesh container should be no more than 23 cm (9 in). Each plant will have a surface spread of 30–60 cm (1–2 ft).
- **Small waterlilies:** these need 23–45 cm (9–18 in) of water over the container's top, with each plant having a 60 cm–1.2 m (2–4 ft) spread on the surface.
- **Medium waterlilies:** these need 30–60 cm (1–2 ft) of water above the container's rim, with each plant having a 1.2–1.5 m (4–5 ft) spread on the water's surface.
- **Vigorous waterlilies:** best restricted to lakes and very large ponds. A water depth of 45–90 cm (18–36 in) is needed. Each plant will have a 1.5–2.4 m (5–8 ft) spread on the surface.

WHEN PLANTING IN A POND

Never plant a waterlily or any other water plant directly in soil in the base of a garden pond; it will make lifting and dividing plants difficult without having to totally drain the pond. Also, when waterlilies are initially bought they may not have long stems and if planted too deeply will suffer. By planting in a plastic-mesh container, which initially can be stood on bricks in the pond's base, the leaves will float on the water's surface. As leaf-stems grow longer, the bricks can be removed. Planting in containers also makes feeding plants easier. These plastic-mesh containers are readily available from garden centres and water-plant specialists.

DANGEROUS INTRODUCTIONS
Never introduce fish, amphibians or plants to your pond that you have not checked as being suitable. And certainly never put anything in your pond that you have mistakenly brought back from a foreign country.

Vegetables

What can I grow?

There is a wide range of vegetables and many are suitable for small gardens (see below). The varieties on sale in greengrocers and supermarkets are often restricted to those that are profitable to commercial growers, whereas when growing your own food it is possible to have varieties that specifically suit the needs of you and your family. It is worth growing a number of different varieties of each vegetable to prolong the harvesting period and to avoid gluts.

Tomatoes in containers

- **Hanging-baskets:** use a 45 cm (18 in) wide, wire-framed basket and line it with polythene. Fill it with equal parts soil-based and peat-based compost; when all risk of frost has passed, plant a bush-type variety such as 'Tumbler'. Plants are naturally bushy and do not need to have sideshoots removed.

- **Growing-bags:** in late spring, plant 3–4 'cordon' types in a large growing-bag. Supports are essential (proprietary types are available). Regularly water and feed plants. Remove sideshoots and pick fruits when ripe.

- **Pots:** in late spring, plant a 'cordon' type in a large pot of loam-based compost. Support the plant with a cane and remove sideshoots.

Vegetables in growing-bags

Several vegetables grow well in growing-bags on a sheltered patio or balcony. Plant as soon as all risk of frost has passed.

- **Bush French beans:** plant six bushy plants. The pods are ready to be picked when, if bent, they snap – usually when 10–15 cm (4–6 in) long.

- **Courgettes (zucchini):** use two plants. Water and feed plants regularly and harvest the courgettes when young and tender. This encourages the development of further courgettes.

- **Lettuces:** grow eight lettuces in a bag.

- **Potatoes:** in early to mid-spring, cut eight, 7.5–10 cm (3–4 in) long, cross-slits in the top and push a tuber of an early variety into each. Cover and water them, then fold back the plastic to exclude light.

VEGETABLES FOR SMALL GARDENS

Many vegetables are quick-growing or need only a small growing space, whereas potatoes, cabbages and cauliflowers are much better in larger plots. Therefore, in small gardens consider the following:

- **Aubergines (eggplants):** these frost-tender vegetables can be grown outdoors in sheltered and warm positions, as well as in growing-bags, large pots, wall-baskets and mangers. Fertile compost is essential; buy established plants and plant as soon as risk of frost has passed.

- **Beetroot:** choose Globe types, which are round and quick-maturing. During spring, form drills 2.5 cm (1 in) deep and 30 cm (1 ft) apart. Sow seeds in clusters of three, 10–15 cm (4–6 in) apart. When the seedlings have formed their first leaves (other than their 'seed' leaves), thin them to one seedling at each position.

- **Carrots:** choose short-rooted varieties (which are finger-like) or those that resemble small golf balls. From mid-spring to the latter part of early summer, sow seeds in drills 12–18 mm (½–¾ in) deep and 15 cm (6 in) apart. Sow seeds thinly and thin seedlings to about 6 cm (2½ in) apart. Refirm soil around the remaining seedlings. When young carrots are large enough to be eaten, pull them up. Twist off the foliage, just above the swollen roots.

- **Courgettes (zucchini):** these are frost-tender plants that resemble small marrows. They can be grown outdoors in fertile, moisture-retentive soil in full sun. Plant when all risk of frost has passed and harvest when 10 cm (4 in) long.

- **Cucumbers (outdoor):** also known as ridge cucumbers, they need a warm, sunny, wind-sheltered position. In mid-spring, dig a hole 30 cm (1 ft) deep and 38 cm (15 in) wide. Fill it with a mixture of friable soil and well-decomposed garden compost. Replace the excavated soil to form a mound. In mid-or late spring in warm areas, or early summer in cold regions, sow three seeds, 18 mm (¾ in) deep, in a small cluster. Water them and cover with a large jam-jar. After germination, remove the jar and when the seedlings have several leaves thin them to leave the strongest seedling in each position. Harvest the cucumbers during mid- and late summer, when they have reached 15–20 cm (6–8 in) in length.

- **French beans:** ideal in small gardens. Choose varieties such as 'Masterpiece', 'Tendergreen' and 'The Prince'. Fertile, moisture-retentive soil is essential to encourage rapid growth. In late spring or early summer, form drills

5 cm (2 in) deep and 45 cm (18 in) apart. Sow individual seeds 7.5–10 cm (3–4 in) apart. From mid-summer onwards, pick the pods when young: they should snap when bent sideways. Do not leave them to become old and tough.

- **Lettuces:** there are several types of lettuce:
  Cabbage types: includes Butterheads (soft-leaved and globular) and Crispheads (round and crisp heads).
  Cos types: upright, with crisp, oblong heads. They take longer to grow than cabbage types, and are slightly more difficult to grow.
  Loose-leaf types: they do not develop a heart; instead, each plant has masses of leaves that can be harvested individually. This type is ideal for small gardens and where only a few leaves are needed at one time.
- **Radishes:** choose summer radishes, such as 'Cherry Belle' (globular), 'French Breakfast' (oblong), 'Red Prince' (globular) and 'Scarlet Globe' (globular). From mid-spring to late summer, sow seeds every two weeks. Form drills 12 mm (½ in) deep and 15 cm (6 in) apart and sow thinly.

When the seedlings are large enough to handle, thin them to 2.5 cm (1 in) apart. Harvest them by pulling up when large enough to be used in salads.

- **Runner beans:** where space is limited, grow these beans on wigwams of poles 1.6–2.1 m (6–7 ft) high. Erect the supports in late spring; sow 2–3 seeds around the base of each pole. Thin the seedlings to one strong plant for each pole. Harvest the pods while still young and tender, as aged pods tend to become tough and stringy.
- **Spring onions:** also known as salad onions and bunching onions, they are ideal for adding to salads. Choose varieties such as 'White Lisbon' and 'Ishikuro'. Dig the soil in winter and in early spring fork and rake it to create a fine tilth. Every two weeks, from early or mid-spring to the early part of mid-summer, sow seeds in drills 12 mm (½ in) deep and 10–13 cm (4–5 in) apart. This produces onions from early summer to early autumn. Use a garden fork to loosen the soil around the plants so that they can be easily pulled up without causing them any damage.

CROP ROTATION

Vegetables can be arranged – through their shared needs – into three groups. Therefore, divide the vegetable garden into three parts. Each part will contain one of the following groupings, which are rotated each year.

Group One

Root crops: beetroot, carrots, parsnips, salsify and scorzonera. Potatoes can also be included here.

Soil preparation: when preparing soil, neither add lime nor dig in manure. Instead, rake in a general fertilizer a couple of weeks before sowing or planting.

Group Two

Brassicas: broccoli, Brussels sprouts, cabbages, cauliflowers, kale, kohl rabi, radishes and swedes.

Soil preparation: dig the soil in winter, add well-decayed manure or garden compost, especially if the soil is lacking humus (decayed organic material, such as farmyard manure and garden compost). If the soil is acid, apply lime, but not at the same time as digging in manure or compost. About two weeks before sowing or planting, rake a general-purpose fertilizer into the soil.

Group Three

Legumes and other vegetables: aubergines (eggplants), beans, capsicums, celery, celeriac, leeks, lettuce, marrows, onions, peas, spinach, sweetcorn and tomatoes.

Soil preparation: when preparing soil in early winter, dig in garden compost or manure. Then, in late winter lime the soil (if it is acid) and, about two weeks before sowing or planting, rake in a general fertilizer.

Culinary herbs

Most herbs are easy to grow, whether in borders or containers. In cottage gardens, they can be closely mixed with other plants, or more ornamentally planted in cartwheel herb gardens and draughtboard designs. In containers, they are ideal in windowboxes and decorative herb pots, as well as pots and troughs on patios and balconies. By far the majority of herbs are hardy, and some, such as mints, grow from year to year until they are too congested.

SIX POPULAR HERBS

Chives Mint

Parsley Sage

Tarragon Thyme

Although there are many culinary herbs, six of them (see below) are especially popular. There are others and they all play a role in adding flavour to food and drinks, as well as being used as garnishes.

- *Allium schoenoprasum* **(Chives):** bulbous, with tubular, onion-flavoured leaves, popular in salads.
- *Artemisia dracunculus* **(French Tarragon):** leaves used to flavour meat and fish, as well as adding to omelettes.
- *Mentha* **spp. (Mints):** several kinds, but the best known one is *Mentha spicata* (Spearmint); they have a variety of culinary uses.
- *Petroselinum crispum* **(Parsley):** popular for garnishing dishes, as well as adding to sauces.
- *Salvia officinalis* **(Sage):** grey-green, wrinkled leaves, used fresh or dried and added to food such as rich meat and poultry; also used in stuffings.
- *Thymus vulgaris* **(Thyme):** well known for its leaves, which are used to flavour food.

GROWING CYCLES OF HERBS

These are diverse and reflect the wide range of garden plants. They include:

- **Annuals:** single-season plants – germinating, flowering and dying within the same year.
- **Biennials:** have a two-year growing and flowering cycle (see pages 48–49).
- **Bulbs:** are swollen stem bases, formed of fleshy, modified scales tightly packed around each other.
- **Herbaceous perennials:** moderately long-term plants which die down to soil level in autumn and send up fresh shoots in spring. Usually need lifting and dividing, and replanting of young plants, every 3–4 years.
- **Shrub-like:** have a woody structure and the ability to live for many years – perhaps ten or more. Some are hardy, while others are slightly tender and in temperate climates may lose some or all of their leaves. Some shrubs are deciduous, and others are evergreen.

HERBS FOR CONTAINERS

Some herbs are especially suited for certain containers – here is a guide to choices that will give assured results. Many of these are illustrated on the opposite page.

Growing-bags
Mentha spp. (Mints); *Salvia officinalis* (Sage), when young

Hanging-baskets
Petroselinum crispum (Parsley); *Thymus vulgaris* (Thyme)

Pots and planters
Allium schoenoprasum (Chives); *Mentha* spp. (Mints); *Ocimum basilicum* (Basil); *Petroselinum crispum* (Parsley); *Rosmarinus officinalis* (Rosemary); *Salvia officinalis* (Sage), when young; *Thymus vulgaris* (Thyme)

Troughs and windowboxes
Allium schoenoprasum (Chives); *Artemisia dracunculus* (French Tarragon); *Mentha* spp. (Mints); *Origanum majorana* (Marjoram)

Tubs
Laurus nobilis (Bay); *Rosmarinus officinalis* (Rosemary); *Salvia officinalis* (Sage)

WHERE TO GROW HERBS

Colour-designed herb gardens

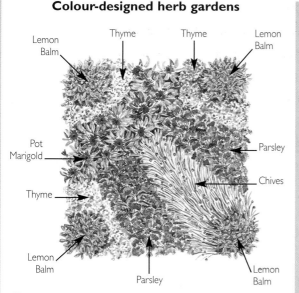

Lemon Balm

Thyme

Thyme

Lemon Balm

Pot Marigold

Parsley

Chives

Thyme

Lemon Balm

Parsley

Lemon Balm

↗ Large herb gardens are superb when planted with flowering and colour-leaved herbs in attractive patterns. Colour-leaved forms of *Salvia officinalis* (Sage) can also be used – there are several superb varieties.

Paved herb gardens

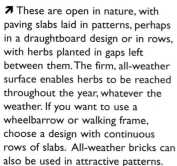

↗ These are open in nature, with paving slabs laid in patterns, perhaps in a draughtboard design or in rows, with herbs planted in gaps left between them. The firm, all-weather surface enables herbs to be reached throughout the year, whatever the weather. If you want to use a wheelbarrow or walking frame, choose a design with continuous rows of slabs. All-weather bricks can also be used in attractive patterns.

Cartwheel herb gardens

➜ Few herb-garden features are as eye-catching as a cartwheel placed on its side on prepared soil and with low-growing herbs planted between the spokes. Even if a cartwheel is not available, the shape of a wheel can be simulated by stones to form the hub, spokes and rim. Further colour can be added – after plants have been put in position – by covering the soil with shingle.

Corner and narrow beds

➜ Many modern gardens have only space for narrow borders, or perhaps a corner bed. Yet this need not be a problem, as the heights and spreads of herbs vary; by choosing suitable types, all spaces can be filled and a magnificent display created. Take care, however, not to use spreading types, such as Mints, unless they are planted in bottomless pots.

Formal herb gardens

↗ These herb gardens are ideal where their surroundings also radiate formality. They have a regular shape and are ideal for fusing with a formal lawn. In shape, the garden can be square, oblong or round, but is usually sectioned into symmetrical parts. Small, low, evergreen hedges, perhaps formed of *Buxus sempervirens* 'Suffruticosa' (Dwarf Box), can be used to unite the herb garden.

Soft fruits

What are soft fruits?

Fruits that are borne on bushes and canes or in the case of strawberries at ground level are known as soft fruits. They do not have such a long life expectancy as tree fruits, but bear fruits much earlier in their lives. Strawberries, for example, if planted in late summer or early autumn will bear a few fruits during the following year, but more during the next season. Regular attention is needed throughout the lives of soft fruit bushes and canes.

Summer-fruiting raspberries are easy to grow and pruning is not complicated.

Harvesting and eating soft fruits

Details of the times for harvesting and eating soft fruits are indicated on page 9.

A QUESTION OF YIELD?

- **Blackberries:** expect yields of 4.5–11.3 kg (10–25 lb) from each plant.
- **Blackcurrants:** expect a yearly yield from each bush of 4.5–6.8 kg (10–15 lb).
- **Gooseberries:** expect a yearly yield from each bush of 2.7–5.5 kg (6–12 lb).
- **Raspberries (summer-fruiting types):** expect yields of 2 kg (4½ lb) for each 90 cm (3 ft) of row.
- **Raspberries (autumn-fruiting types):** expect yields of 680 g (1½ lb) for each 90 cm (3 ft) of row.
- **Redcurrants:** expect a yearly yield from each bush of 4.5 kg (10 lb).
- **Strawberries:** an established plant will produce 170–680 g (6 oz–1½ lb) of fruit each year.

STRAWBERRIES IN CONTAINERS

Hanging-baskets

Use a seed-raised variety and buy young plants in late spring or early summer. Put three plants in a large hanging-basket; do not place them outside until all risk of frost has passed.

Strawberry planters

These have cupped holes in their sides, in which plants can be planted – as well as in the top. Ensure good drainage; roll a piece of wire-netting (slightly less than the depth of the planter) to form a tube about 7.5 cm (3 in) wide. Insert this into the planter and fill with large pebbles. Fill the planter with loam-based compost to level with the lowest cupped hole, and put a plant in it. Continue filling and planting; lastly, put plants in the top. Thoroughly water the compost.

Strawberry planter

GROWING HABITS OF SOFT FRUITS

These vary widely, such as:
- **Strawberries:** the most popular soft fruit, with a low, bushy and trailing habit; once planted they can be left in position for 3–4 years. Plant them in soil at ground level. They can also be planted in containers (see above).
- **Blackcurrants:** bush-like, with several stems arising from the ground.
- **Red- and whitecurrants:** bush-like, and with a short stem ('leg') that unites the branches with the roots.
- **Gooseberries:** bush-like and forming a permanent framework of branches; similarly to redcurrants, bushes have a 'leg'.
- **Raspberries:** cane-like structures, requiring support from tiers of wires.
- **Blackberries:** similar to raspberries.

SOFT FRUITS FOR SMALL GARDENS

Blackcurrants

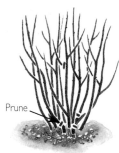

Easily grown bush fruit, with shoots growing directly from soil-level. Fruits are borne on shoots produced during the previous year. As soon as the fruits have been picked, cut out all stems that produced them. This leaves young shoots (produced during that season) to bear fruits during the following year. Bushes grow to about 1.5 m (5 ft) high.

Prune

Pruning is tackled immediately the fruits have been picked.

Blackberries

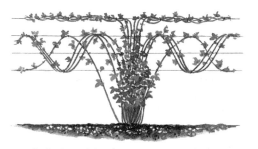

Blackberries need tiers of strong wires to support their canes.

Popular cane fruit, needing support from a framework of tiered wires, 30 cm (1 ft) apart from 90 cm (3 ft) to 2.1 m (7 ft) high. These are stretched between strong posts, in full sun or light shade. Immediately after picking, cut out all fruited canes to ground level and tie in young ones to the wires. Space the plants 2.4–3.6 m (8–12 ft) apart, depending on vigour.

Gooseberries

Usually grown as bushes, with fruits borne on a permanent framework of shoots supported by a single, leg-like stem. Bushes are 90 cm–1.5 m (3–5 ft) high. Prune established bushes between early winter and early spring, cutting back by half new growths at the ends of stems. Also cut back sideshoots to 5 cm (2 in) long.

Prune gooseberry bushes between early winter and early spring.

Raspberries

Raspberries need tiers of strong wires tensioned between posts.

Summer-fruiting types: popular cane fruits, needing a supporting framework of tiered wires, 30–38 cm (12–15 in) apart to 1.8 m (6 ft) high. These are stretched between strong posts, in full sun. Avoid frost pockets. Immediately after picking, cut out all fruited canes to ground level and tie in young canes to the supporting wires. Fertile, moisture-retentive soil is essential to encourage the yearly production of new canes.

Autumn-fruiting types: fruits are similar to those of summer-fruiting types, but produced from late summer to mid-autumn. Autumn-fruiting raspberries bear fruits on the tips of shoots produced earlier during the same season; for this reason, pruning is easier than for summer-fruiting types. In late winter of each year, cut all canes to ground level; in spring, fresh shoots appear and these bear fruits later in the same year. Plants usually remain productive for 7–10 years.

Red- and whitecurrants

Popular fruit, grown on bushes 1.5–1.8 m (5–6 ft) high and wide. Bushes have a permanent framework of shoots supported by a single, leg-like stem. Bushes remain productive for 10–15 years.

Red and white currant bushes are grown on short stems.

Strawberries

Summer-fruiting types: popular fruit for growing in beds or containers (see left). For a worthwhile crop, you should plant at least 20 plants in a bed, and be prepared to replant them every 3–4 years.

Tree fruits

What are tree fruits?

These are fruits that are borne on trees, or specially trained forms of trees such as cordons, espaliers and fans. They all have a permanent, woody structure and therefore have a much longer life-span than soft fruits. For this reason, great care is needed in their selection if there is not to be a disaster in later years. And, for gardeners who are not as active as they were in earlier years, pruning and training cordons, espaliers and fans is easier than climbing stepladders.

Peaches and nectarines need the comfort of a warm wall.

HARVESTING AND EATING TREE FRUITS

For details of the times for harvesting and eating tree fruits, see page 8. When picking these fruits, care is essential to prevent them being bruised.

- **Apples and pears:** test for picking by cupping individual fruits and gently lifting and slightly twisting the stalk. If the stalk readily parts from the branch, the fruit is ready to be picked.
- **Peaches and nectarines:** pick fruits when the flesh around the stalk is soft; pick as for apples and pears.
- **Plums:** fruits are ready for picking when they easily part from the tree – the stalk usually remains on the tree. Take care not to squeeze and bruise them.
- **Sweet cherries:** these are left on the tree until they are ripe. Ripeness can be checked by picking a few fruits and tasting them. However, pick cracked fruits immediately.

TREE FORMS

The shapes and sizes of trees bearing fruits vary widely, from dwarf trees at only 1.8 m (6 ft) high to vigorous ones some 7.5 m (25 ft) in height. In addition to a tree-like structure (whatever its size), there are 'trained' types such as cordons, espaliers and fans (see the Glossary for full details). Clearly, for most home gardens – and especially those with only a restricted space for tree fruits – small trees, as well as cordons, espaliers and fans, are the best choice. Unfortunately, these choices do not apply to all tree fruits.

APPLES IN TUBS AND POTS

Apples are a popular tree fruit to grow in a container, but there are a few essential considerations:

- Wooden tubs or large terracotta pots are essential, at least 38 cm (15 in) deep and wide. Place broken pieces of clay pots in them to create good drainage, and use soil-based compost.
- Use dwarfing rootstocks such as M27 or M9. Without these, growing apples in containers is not practical.
- To ensure pollination (and the subsequent development of fruit), choose a 'family' tree, where 3–4 different yet compatible varieties have been grafted onto one rootstock. Alternatively, it is necessary to plant – in separate containers – several compatible varieties.
- Buy a two-year-old tree and plant and support it with a strong stake.
- It is best trained as a pyramid, which means in winter cutting back the leading shoots to about 15 cm (6 in) from where it developed from the trunk. Also cut back sideshoots near the plant's top to 15–20 cm (6–8 in) from the trunk, and those near the base to 25–30 cm (10–12 in) from the trunk.
- During the second winter, cut back all branches to 15–20 cm (6–8 in) from where they developed during the previous growing period.
- During the first year, allow 2–3 fruits to develop; in later years, expect about 4.5 kg (10 lb) of fruit each year.

Varieties to try include:

- **'Blenheim Orange':** dessert and culinary variety; pick apples in mid-autumn; ready for eating from late autumn to early winter.
- **'Discovery':** dessert variety; pick apples in late summer; ready for eating during late summer and early autumn.
- **'Egremont Russet':** dessert variety; pick apples in early autumn; ready for eating from mid-autumn to early winter.
- **'James Grieve':** dessert variety; pick apples in early autumn; ready for eating in early and mid-autumn.
- **'Sunset':** dessert variety; pick apples in early autumn; ready for eating from mid-autumn to early winter.

TREE FRUITS FOR SMALL GARDENS

Apples

Prune

Apple trees need yearly pruning during their dormant period.

In confined areas, grow them either as espaliers or cordons against walls; alternatively, as dwarf pyramids or dwarf bushes. Dwarfing apple rootstocks help to keep trees small, and include M27 (eventually growing 1.5–1.8 m (5–6 ft) high) and M9 (maturing 2.4–3 m (8–10 ft) high). To ensure pollination (and subsequent development of fruit), compatible varieties planted close by are essential. Check with the nursery or garden centre about compatible varieties that ensure pollination. However, where only one tree is possible, choose a 'family' tree, where 3–4 varieties have been grafted onto it. Always buy a 'family' tree from a reputable nursery.

Pears

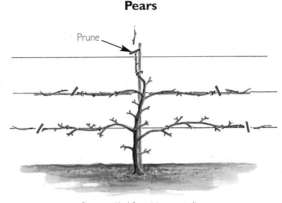

Prune

Pears are ideal for training as espaliers.

In confined areas, grow pears either as espaliers, 4.5 m (15 ft) apart, or cordons 75 cm (30 in) apart. Pollination partners are essential and, in a small garden, the easiest way to overcome this problem is to plant a 'family' tree, where several different varieties have been grafted onto the same tree. Usually, there are three different varieties.

Nectarines

These are smooth-skinned forms of the peach. There are several varieties, but all are less hardy than peaches and therefore best grown as a fan-trained tree against a warm, wind-sheltered wall. Grow it on the St Julien A rootstock.

Fan-trained and grown against a warm, wind-sheltered wall.

Peaches

Succulent fruits with somewhat rough, hairy skins. In a small garden, fan-trained trees are best, positioned against a warm, wind-sheltered wall. For a small garden, use Pixy rootstock, with 2.4 m (8 ft) between trees. Although slightly hardier than nectarines, peaches nevertheless need a warm position.

Plums

Like sweet cherries, plum trees have a history of growing very large and not being suitable for a small garden. However, dwarfing rootstocks are now available and these can restrict a tree's height to 4.5 m (15 ft) or less. Unfortunately, they are not suitable for cold and exposed areas as they flower earlier than most tree fruits.

Plums can be grown as bushes, pyramids or half-standards (as illustrated here).

Sweet cherries

In earlier years, these were far too vigorous for an average-sized garden, but relatively recently dwarfing forms have become available. These can restrict the height of a tree to 2.1 m (7 ft), and fan-trained types to 2.4 m (8 ft) high. Self-fertile varieties are also available and this has helped to make cherries much easier to grow.

Pests

What problems do they cause?

There are many types of pest, from those that wholly or partly inhabit the soil to ones that infest leaves, stems and flowers, as well as fruits, vegetables and herbs. Some pests cause damage through their chewing and rasping habits, while others suck sap and produce further debilitation by transmitting viruses from one plant to another. Rabbits and squirrels cause damage to bark and trunks, while birds eat and tear buds on fruit trees.

Caterpillars

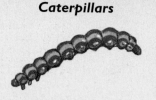

The larvae of moths and butterflies, they infest garden plants, eating and chewing soft stems, leaves and flowers.

What to do: pick off caterpillars and spray with an insecticide as soon as they – or the damage – is seen.

Cockchafer grubs

Often known as 'May bugs' and 'June bugs', both larvae and adult beetles attack plants. Adult beetles feed and fly during early and mid-summer, chewing flowers and leaves of many ornamental plants. The dirty, creamy-white larvae, about 3 cm (1¼ in) long, live in the soil, chewing roots. They are usually seen in a characteristically curled-up position.

What to do: whenever possible, pick off and destroy adults and larvae. Also dust the leaves with an insecticide.

Cutworms

Larvae of certain moths. They are mainly active at night, chewing seedlings and plants at ground level, causing them to collapse and giving the impression of being cut down.

What to do: when preparing new flower or vegetable beds, dig the soil in winter and pick off and destroy the larvae. Remove weeds and regularly hoe around plants throughout summer to disturb the soil. Also dust the soil with a pesticide.

Earwigs

Pernicious and omnipresent pests. They clamber into plants, damaging soft stems, leaves and flowers. They especially like dark and secluded places.

What to do: pick them off and destroy, or trap in pots filled with straw and inverted on the tops of bamboo canes. Each morning, empty and destroy the earwigs. Also spray or dust with a pesticide.

Greenfly (aphids)

Also known as aphids and aphis, they suck sap from leaves, stems, shoots and flowers, causing discoloration and debilitation, as well as spreading viruses. At the same time, they excrete honeydew, which attracts ants and encourages the presence of sooty mould, a black and unsightly fungus. Blackfly are related to greenfly and are just as pernicious.

What to do: spray with an insecticide as soon as damage or pests are seen. Repeat sprayings are necessary.

Leatherjackets

Tough-skinned, fat and legless grubs of craneflies, also known as daddy-long-legs. They live in the soil, chewing roots and causing either death or wilting of plants. They are most troublesome on land newly converted from grassland.

What to do: deeply dig the soil in winter to expose the grubs to birds and frost, as well as to the drying effects of wind and sun. Pick off and destroy them, and dust around plants with a pesticide.

Millipedes

Unlike centipedes, which have a single pair of legs on each body segment, these have two. They are therefore slower and less agile, but better equipped to climb plants and to chew them, from young roots, tubers, bulbs and stems to seedlings. They soon devastate plants.

What to do: remove all rubbish and dust with a pesticide. Hoeing around plants also helps to ensure that they cannot hide in surface soil.

Slugs

These are nature's stealth pests, mainly appearing at night and chewing plants, especially when the weather is mild and damp.

What to do: use slug baits, but ensure that they are not accessible to pets and wildlife. Scattering sharp sand or broken eggshells around plants deters them. 'Slippery tapes' wrapped around pots and tubs also help to prevent them reaching plants.

Snails

Like slugs, they are pests of the night, chewing and tearing leaves and stems.

What to do: use baits in a similar way as for slugs. After a shower of rain they often appear in large numbers.

Thrips

Minute insects, often known as thunderflies, they infest flowers and leaves, piercing and sucking the tissues and causing silvery streaking and mottling. They frequently appear in vast numbers.

What to do: dust or spray plants with an insecticide.

Whiteflies

Small, white, moth-like flies, closely related to aphids, that live mainly on the undersides of leaves, sucking sap and excreting honeydew that encourages the presence of ants and a black, sooty mould.

What to do: spray with an insecticide as soon as they are seen, but control is difficult and repeat spraying is essential.

Woodlice

Also known as slaters and pillbugs, these are hard-coated pests that live in dark, damp places and come out at night to feed on stems, roots and leaves. As well as chewing plants at soil level, they attack plants in tubs, pots and growing-bags on patios. They also climb walls and infest mangers and windowboxes.

What to do: remove all rubbish under which they can hide, and dust the soil with a pesticide.

Chemical controls

There are two types of chemicals used to kill insects and other pests:

- **Contact insecticides:** sprayed at the first sign of a pest attack when, by contact, they kill the insect or make the plant's surface toxic.
- **Systemic insecticides:** chemicals enter a plant's sap stream and make it toxic to insects; especially useful when combating sap-sucking pests such as greenfly.

For safety, when using garden chemicals, see page 73.

BENEFICIAL INSECTS

There are many of them, including capsid bugs, dragonflies, lacewings, ichneumon flies and chalcids, but the best known are:

- **Braconid flies:** lay eggs in caterpillars, parasitizing and killing them.
- **Green lacewings:** they appear delicate, but adults and larvae are voracious eaters of aphids and other soft-bodied insect pests.
- **Ground beetles:** natural predators, with agile, well-armoured larvae; both adults and larvae destroy large numbers of small insects, especially at night. They also eat large numbers of cabbage root fly eggs, as well as root aphids. The violet ground beetle attacks slugs.
- **Hoverflies:** characterized by hovering in the air, these flies are important predators of aphids. They also help to control red spider mites on fruit trees, and caterpillars of the lackey moth.
- **Ladybirds:** many species, with different colours and numbers of spots. Both larvae and adults are predators, eating vast numbers of aphids as well as mealy bugs, thrips, mites and scale insects. Each larvae of the two-spot ladybird can eat 15–20 aphids a day.
- **Rove beetles:** large family of soil-living beetles, including the devil's coach horse. Both adults and larvae of rove beetles are predators and voraciously consume lettuce root aphids, strawberry aphids and red spider mites.

OTHER BENEFICIAL CREATURES

- **Centipedes:** active, eating slugs, woodlice, mites, leatherjackets, grubs and other insects.
- **Frogs and toads:** amphibians with a liking for slugs.
- **Hedgehogs:** voracious appetite for slugs, beetles, earwigs, cutworms and millipedes.
- **Shrews:** very small mammals with big appetites for insects, and it is claimed that some eat their own bodyweight of food in a single day.
- **Slow-worms:** legless lizards, eating millipedes, earwigs, slugs, beetles and caterpillars.

Diseases

(see below)

Are these a major problem?

There are many kinds of plant disease (see below) that can soon make plants unsightly, often eventually causing death. Unless plants are regularly checked (both above and below leaves, as well as stems and flowers), the infection can become uncontrollable. All that you can then do is dig up and burn the plants, or cut out all the infected parts. In additon, there are physiological disorders (which are not caused by diseases, but by environmental influences); these include sun scald on tomatoes.

TYPES OF PLANT DISEASE

Plant diseases fall into four main categories:
- **Fungal diseases:** mainly parasitical, with the fungus feeding on the host plant. Well-known ones include damping off on seedlings (encouraged by damp and badly ventilated greenhouse) and black spot on roses.
- **Bacterial diseases:** individual bacteria are some of the smallest living organisms. Examples in plants include blackleg of potatoes, crown gall and gladiolus scab.
- **Rusts:** types of fungus that produces rust-red or brown, raised areas on leaves, such as when infecting carnations. Rusts have complicated life cycles.
- **Viruses:** these live in the sap of plants, stunting and deforming growth. They are mainly spread by sap-sucking insects, and when infected plants are vegetatively propagated, such as by cuttings.

HOW TO AVOID GETTING PESTS AND DISEASES

- Before buying, check plants to ensure they are free from pests and diseases – look above and below leaves, as well as around flowers and young shoots. Always buy from reputable sources.
- Never leave rubbish lying around on the soil as it encourages the presence of pests and disease. Clear it away and either place on a compost heap or burn (if seriously contaminated with pests and diseases).
- Keep the soil free from weeds, as many of them harbour pests and diseases.
- Thoroughly prepare the soil before planting and sowing. Deep digging both ensures good drainage and aeration throughout the soil, as well as exposing soil pests such as cockchafer grubs to birds.

Physiological disorders of tomatoes

- **Blossom drop:** flowers wither and break off. Keep the compost evenly moist and mist-spray the plants.
- **Blotchy ripening:** skin remains orange or yellow and fails to ripen. Apply potash and avoid high temperatures.
- **Dry set:** fruitlets cease to develop when the size of match-heads. Mist-spray plants several times a day.
- **Split fruit:** outdoors and in greenhouses, skin splits. Keep the compost evenly moist.
- **Sun scald:** papery, light brown depressions on sides of fruits in greenhouses and facing the glass. Provide shading.

Black spot

Fungal disease of roses, causing unsightly black spots on leaves. When the disease is severe, the spots merge to form large, blackened areas. The young leaves are infected first.

What to do: as soon as the disease is seen, spray the leaves with a fungicide. Also remove and burn fallen, infected leaves to prevent the disease spreading.

Damping off

Mainly a disease of young seedlings in greenhouses. It is exacerbated by badly drained compost and high humidity. Seedlings appear to collapse at compost level, due to a withering of the stem at that point.

What to do: use well-drained compost, water carefully to prevent waterlogging, and avoid high humidity.

Grey mould

Often known as *botrytis*, it creates fluffy, mould-like growths on flowers, soft stems and leaves.

What to do: cut off and destroy infected parts (often entire plants, if infection is severe). Increase ventilation and use a fungicide.

Peach leaf curl

Fungal disease that infects almonds, apricots, nectarines and peaches, as well as ornamental trees related to them. Infected leaves are first seen in spring, soon after unfolding, with pale greenish-yellow areas. Later, they assume deep crimson shading; leaves thicken and become coated in a white bloom. Leaves eventually fall off.

What to do: spray with a proprietary fungicide in late winter, early spring and just before leaves fall in autumn.

Rose rust

A common and difficult rust to eradicate. It is an unsightly disease, with orange swellings on the undersides of leaves. In late summer, they turn black. New shoots become reddish and shrivel.

What to do: spray plants regularly, especially if this rust is a widespread problem in your area. Feeding plants with a balanced fertilizer in early summer helps to keep roses healthy.

Chemical controls

There are two types of chemicals used to prevent and control plant diseases:

- **Contact fungicides:** sprayed on plants anticipated to be infected by a disease, when they kill germinating fungal spores and prevent further infection. However, they have little effect on established fungal growths.

- **Systemic fungicides:** absorbed by plants and enter the sap stream, when they are able to kill fungi within a plant's tissue.

Silver leaf

Mainly a problem of apricots, cherries, nectarines, peaches and ornamental cherries. This fungal disease enters a tree through a wound or pruning cut. Branches become infected, producing silvered leaves and brown staining on infected wood. Shoots eventually die back.

What to do: prune only in spring or summer and paint the cuts with a fungicidal paint. Feeding plants aids partial recovery.

Viruses

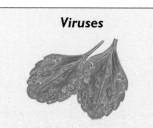

Infect many plants, usually causing discoloration and distortion. Leaves may have white streaks.

What to do: there is no cure – you must throw away and burn infected plants and spray with insecticides to kill sap-sucking insects, such as greenfly, that spread them.

Safety first with garden chemicals

Chemicals sprayed on plants in gardens are lethal to pests and therefore must be treated with respect.

- Carefully follow the manufacturer's instructions. Do not be tempted to use chemicals at higher than recommended concentrations as they will not be more effective, and may even damage plants.

- Do not spray near garden ponds, or where family rabbits and guinea pigs are kept and especially if they are in open runs on lawns.

- Do not mix two different chemicals, unless recommended.

- Before using, check that the chemical will not damage specific plants.

- Keep all chemicals away from children and pets, and do not transfer chemicals into bottles that children might believe to be a refreshing drink.

- Do no use the same equipment for both weedkillers and insecticides.

- Thoroughly wash all spraying equipment after use, and store in a place not frequented by children and animals.

- If you have an accident, seek medical advice immediately – and take along the chemical and its packaging.

- When spraying vegetables, check that the chemical is suitable for food crops, and that the recommended period between spraying and harvesting is observed.

Cankers on trees

Canker is a general term for any kind of open wound on shrubs and trees, as well as other plants. Cankers usually appear as sunken, deformed areas on limbs and trunks and are cause by a number of different fungi. Examination indicates successive layers of dead tissue, with the tree making yearly attempts to grow over the originally damaged and infected area.

Bacterial canker is a serious disease of fruiting and ornamental cherries, plums and peaches. Infection is likely to occur during autumn and winter, when spores enter wounds. Therefore, only prune these trees in spring or summer. Paint wounds with a fungicidal tree paint.

What to do: spray plants regularly, especially if this rust is a widespread problem in your local area. Feeding plants with a balanced fertilizer in early summer helps to keep roses healthy.

Jargon-busting glossary

Every hobby, profession and pursuit in life has its own vocabulary and terminology, often steeped in history and used to foster rapid and easy discussion between like-minded people. Therefore, it is not surprising that an aged pursuit such as gardening has gathered its own terms which often cause confusion to novice gardeners. Some of these terms have a botanical heritage and refer to parts of plants and their functions. Here are many of the most widely heard terms.

Acid soil Soil which has a pH of less than pH 7.0 (see pH).

Air layering Method of propagation, encouraging roots to form on a stem. Often used on houseplants such as *Ficus elastica* (Rubber Plant).

Alkaline soil Soil which has a pH of more than pH 7.0 (see pH).

Annuals Plants that grow from seed, flower and die within the same year. However, many plants that are not strictly annuals are treated as such. For example, *Tropaeolum peregrinum* (Canary Creeper) is a half-hardy, short-lived perennial usually grown as a hardy annual; *Cobaea scandens* (Cathedral Bells) is a half-hardy perennial usually grown as a half-hardy annual; *Caiophora laterita* 'Frothy' is a biennial or short-lived perennial usually grown as a half-hardy annual.

Anther The male part of a flower that produces pollen.

Anvil secateurs Type of secateurs, where one blade cuts against a firm, metal surface.

arborescens Having a tree-like nature.

Asexual Non-sexual; frequently used to refer to increasing plants by cuttings and other vegetative methods, including division, grafting and budding.

Balled plants Describes a way in which plants often used to be sold. They are mainly conifers or small evergreen shrubs with hessian tightly wrapped around the rootball, and usually sold during late summer and early autumn, or in spring. When the trend to sell plants growing in containers was introduced several decades ago, the number of plants sold as 'balled' types rapidly diminished.

Bamboo Collective name for a wide range of plants in the grass family. They have stiff canes (some attractively coloured or shaped) and beautiful leaves (some brightly coloured and variegated).

Bare-rooted plants Deciduous shrubs or trees dug up from a nursery bed in winter, when they are bare of leaves, for despatch to gardeners and for subsequent planting while they are still dormant.

Barrels Wooden containers used during earlier years to transport all manner of materials, including beer, flour, tobacco and gunpowder. They range from a pin (20 litres/4½ gallons) to a butt (490 litres/108 gallons). Today, barrels are either cut in half to form tubs, or left intact and drilled with 5 cm (2 in) wide holes so that plants such as strawberries can be grown in them.

Biennials Plants that have a two-year growing and flowering cycle. Seeds are sown in nursery beds in late spring or early summer, and planted in borders in late summer or early autumn. They flower during the following year.

Blanching (1) Sometimes used to help herbs retain their colour prior to drying. It involves dipping them in boiling water for a few seconds. (2) Both trench celery and leeks are blanched by earthing up soil around their stems as they grow to keep them white.

Bolting Describes a plant that prematurely develops seeds, rather than continuing normal growth. Bolting is usually caused by drought, hot weather or exceptionally poor soil.

Bottom heat The warming of a rooting medium from below.

Bouquet garni (pl. *bouquets garnis*) Bunch of herbs, tied together or wrapped in cheesecloth, and used to season food including soups, stews and sauces.

Bud Tightly packed and closed immature shoot or flower.

Budding Uniting a bud of a varietal part with a rootstock of known vigour and quality.

Bulbs Formed of overlapping, fleshy, modified leaves that create a food-storage organ; when given the right conditions, they develop leaves and flowers. Many spring-flowering plants, such as hyacinths and daffodils, are bulbs. Onions and garlic are also bulbous.

Bulbils Small, immature bulbs found around the bases of some bulbs. They can be detached, sown and encouraged to form roots. Some leaves produce bulbils.

Bypass secateurs Type of secateur, where one blade crosses the other. Also known as parrot-type and cross-over secateurs.

Callus Tissue that forms over a wound, usually creating a raised, ridged surface.

Cambium Layer of growth and division just below the bark of woody plants such as shrubs and trees. When grafting, the cambium on both parts must unite.

Cartwheel herb garden Method of arranging herbs, as if planted between the spokes of a cartwheel. If a cartwheel is not available, it can be simulated by stones to form the rim, spokes and hub.

Climbers Plants (whether woody, herbaceous or with an annual growth cycle) that have a natural tendency to climb.

Climbing roses These have larger flowers than rambling types and are borne singly or in small clusters; they generally have the ability to repeat flowering after their first period of bloom.

Clone One of a group of identical plants that have been raised vegetatively from a single, original plant.

Clove Segment of a garlic bulb.

Columnar Upright and narrow. Often used to describe some conifers.

Compost (1) Mixture in which cuttings are inserted, seeds sown and plants replanted or potted. (2) Decomposed vegetable material, better known as garden compost.

Container gardening Growing plants – from summer-flowering bedding plants to climbers, shrubs, conifers and trees – in containers, perhaps on a patio, terrace, courtyard, balcony or verandah.

Container-grown plants Plants growing in containers in nurseries and garden centres, ready for sale. They range from alpine plants to climbers, trees, shrubs and conifers. These plants can be planted at any time of the year, when the soil and weather are suitable.

Cordon Fruit tree (usually an apple or pear), although it can be a soft fruit such as a red- or whitecurrant, that is trained and pruned to form one, two, three or four stems. Most are trained at a 45° angle, although some are upright.

Courtyards Originally, open areas surrounded by buildings or walls, perhaps inside a castle. Nowadays, they are paved areas at the rear of a building and surrounded by a wall.

Crocks Pieces of broken clay pots used to cover drainage holes in pots and other containers. They are placed concave side downwards. Mainly used when repotting plants into clay pots.

Culinary Relating to cooking and the kitchen.

Cultivar Plant raised in cultivation, rather than appearing naturally without any interference from man. Properly, the vast majority of varieties should be known as

cultivars, but 'variety' is the better-known term and is often seen in books, as well as being used in general conversation.

Cutting Severed part of a plant that is encouraged to form roots as a method of propagation.

Deadheading Removal of faded flowerheads to prevent the formation of seeds and to encourage a plant to direct its energies into producing more flowers.

Deciduous Shrubs, trees and woody climbers – and few conifers – that shed their leaves in autumn and produce a fresh array in spring. A few slightly tender evergreens also lose some of their leaves during cold weather.

Dibber (dibble) Pencil-like tool with a slightly rounded end. It is used to transfer seedlings to wider spacings in seed-trays (flats), and to insert cuttings into compost in pots and seed-trays. Larger and thicker dibbers are used to plant young vegetable plants such as leeks, cabbages and cauliflowers in soil in a vegetable plot.

Dibble See Dibber.

Digging, double Digging soil to the depth of two spade blades, 50–60 cm (20–24 in) deep. Although formerly popular, double digging is now only undertaken when land is being converted from grass land to a garden plot, or where the land is compacted and drainage poor.

Digging, single Digging soil to the depth of a spade's blade, 25–30 cm (10–12 in). This is the usual method of digging and performed in late autumn or winter, when the soil's surface is free of vegetation. It is usually undertaken annually in vegetable gardens, hardy-annual borders and borders solely planted with summer-flowering bedding plants.

Division Vegetative method of propagation, involving dividing roots. It is often performed on herbaceous plants with fibrous roots.

Dormant Resting period in a plant's life, normally in late autumn and winter in temperate regions, when a plant makes no noticeable growth. It usually refers to deciduous trees and shrubs.

Drip-tray Integral with some plastic-type hanging-baskets to prevent water dripping on floors and plants beneath.

Edible landscaping North American term for growing herbs, vegetables and fruit in medleys with flowers and in an informal manner.

Ericaceous Describes plants belonging to the Ericaceae family, including heathers, heaths, ericas and daboecias. Most of them grow best in acid soil.

Espalier Fruit tree trained so that its branches form tiers, usually supported by a framework of wires secured to posts at both ends and stretched between them.

Essential oil Volatile oil, usually having the characteristic odour of the plant from which it is derived, and used to make perfumes and flavourings.

Evergreen Plants that appear to retain their leaves throughout the year and therefore are always green. However, they regularly lose leaves, while producing others. Some shrubs, trees and conifers are evergreen.

Eye Growth bud on a tuber, or a bud on a stem.

Eye cuttings Method of increasing grapevines.

F1 First filial generation, the result of a cross between two pure-bred parents.

Fan-trained Method of growing and training fruit trees, mainly against walls but also with the arms of the fan secured to horizontal wires stretched between posts. Many fruit trees are trained in this way, including apples, pears, plums, cherries, nectarines, peaches and apricots.

Fertilization Sexual union of a male and female cell.

Fines herbes French term for finely chopped herbs. They are used fresh or dried, as seasonings and to flavour sauces.

Flat See Seed-tray.

Flower Specialized part of a seed-bearing plant and concerned with reproduction.

Fluid sowing Mixing seeds with a gel in a plastic bag and squeezing it along a drill. It helps seeds to retain moisture around seeds while waiting to germinate.

Form Loose and non-botanical term referring to a variation within a particular species.

Friable Refers to fine and crumbly surface soil.

Fruit Botanically, a mature ovary (female part of a flower) bearing ripe seeds. Fruits can be soft and fleshy, or dry.

Garnish To use herbs, either whole or chopped, to enhance the appearance of food and to add further flavours.

Genera Plural of genus.

Genus Group of species with common botanical characteristics.

Germination Process that occurs within a seed when given adequate moisture, air and warmth. The seedcoat ruptures and a seed leaf (or leaves) grows up and towards the light. At the same time, a root develops. However, to most gardeners, germination is when they see seed leaves appearing through the surface of soil or compost.

Glaucous Blue or grey-green, and usually used to describe leaves and stems.

Goottee layering Also known as 'marcottage' and used to encourage roots to develop on stems, usually shrubs and trees.

Grafting Uniting of a varietal part of a plant with roots of known vigour.

Growing-bags Originally introduced to grow tomatoes on disease-infected soil, but now widely used as homes for many summer-flowering plants, as well as herbs and some vegetables, such as lettuces.

Half-hardy annuals Plants sown in gentle warmth early in the year and later planted outdoors when the weather improves and is free from frost.

Half-ripe cuttings Formed of semi-ripe shoots. Also known as semi-ripe cuttings and semi-mature cuttings.

Hardening off Gradual acclimatizing of tender plants (often half-hardy annuals) to outside conditions. Garden frames are used for this purpose.

Hardy Describes a plant that is able to survive winter outdoors in a temperate climate.

Hardy annuals Plant sown directly into soil outdoors, where seeds germinate and plants grow and produce flowers. In late summer or early autumn, plants die.

Heath Botanically, types of ericaceous plants such as *Erica ciliaris* (Dorset Heath) and *Erica tetralix* (Cross-leaved Heath).

Heel cuttings Vegetative method of increasing woody plants. When forming half-ripe cuttings, part of an older shoot (known as a heel) is left attached to their bases.

Heeling-in Temporarily covering the roots of bare-rooted deciduous trees and shrubs while they are waiting to be planted. It helps to keep the roots moist and cool.

Herbaceous Describes a plant that dies down to soil level in autumn or early winter, after the completion of each season's growth. Fresh shoots appear in spring.

Herbal Book containing information about medicinal and culinary herbs, their uses and properties.

Hormone Chemical that influences the growth and development of a plant. Hormone rooting powders are often used to encourage cuttings to form roots.

H-stake Method of supporting standard trees, using two vertical stakes, each inserted about 30 cm (1 ft) from the trunk. A further, but shorter, stake is secured across the top, about 15 cm (6 in) below the lowest branch; the trunk is secured to it.

Hybrid Plant resulting from a cross between two distinct varieties, species or genera.

Internode Part of a stem between two leaf-joints.

Jardinière Large, decorative stand or pot used to display plants.

Laciniate Botanical description, meaning fringed and usually used to describe the edges and outlines of leaves or flowers.

Layering Vegetative method of increasing plants (usually shrubs and woody climbers) by lowering stems and shallowly burying and securing them in the ground. By twisting, bending or slitting them at the point where buried, the flow or sap is restricted and roots encouraged to form. When new growth appears at the top of the shoot, the layer can be severed from the parent plant and planted into a nursery bed or directly into a border.

Leader Main stem – or several – of trees and shrubs.

Leaf-petiole cuttings Cuttings formed of a leaf and its leaf-stem (petiole).

Leaf-square cuttings Created by cutting a leaf into small squares that can be inserted into compost and encouraged to form roots.

Leaf-stem cuttings Formed of a piece of stem and leaf.

Leaf-triangle cuttings Created by cutting a leaf into small triangles that can be inserted into compost and encouraged to form roots.

Loam-based compost Formed mainly of topsoil, with the addition of sharp sand, peat and fertilizers. The soil is partially sterilized.

Loppers Long-handled secateurs, used to cut thick shoots. They have either a bypass or an anvil-cutting action.

Manger Similar to a wire-framed wall-basket, but with a wider metal framework. It is secured to a wall.

Medicinal herbs Herbs that have curative and healing powers derived from roots, stems, leaves and flowers.

Mist propagation Method of regularly covering cuttings with a fine mist spray of water to keep them cool, reduce transpiration and to encourage rapid rooting.

Mulching Covering the soil around plants – from alpines to herbaceous plants, trees and shrubs – with an organic material (such as well-decayed manure or garden compost) or inorganic materials such as shingle and plastic sheeting. These help to keep the soil cool and damp, and to suppress the growth of weeds.

Node Position at which leaves, stems and sideshoots arise. It is usually slightly swollen.

Nosegay Earlier term for a bunch of fragrant, attractive flowers; still occasionally used. Also known as a posy.

Oblique stake Method of supporting the trunk of a tree. A stake is inserted into the ground at an angle of about 45°, so that its top bisects the trunk. The trunk is then tied to the stake. Ensure that the top of the stake faces into the prevailing wind.

Palmate Botanical term used to describe leaves that resemble the shape of a hand.

Parrot secateurs Early name for bypass or cross-over secateurs, where one blade crosses another.

Partially evergreen Describes shrubs that remain evergreen in most climates, but in cold winters may lose some or all of their leaves.

Patio The Spanish used this term to describe an inner court, open to the sky and surrounded by a building. The surrounding walls helped to keep the patio cool and private. The term was introduced by the Spanish to North America, where it has been corrupted to mean any paved area around or at the side of a dwelling.

Peat-based compost Formerly, mainly formed of peat, with the addition of fertilizers. However, the continued removal of peat from peat beds has put at risk the lives of many insects, birds and animals; therefore, where possible use other composts.

Perlite Moisture-retentive material often added to compost to assist in the retention of moisture.

Petal Part of a flower and, botanically, a modified leaf. Usually coloured and very attractive, it creates a landing platform for pollinating insects. When in bud it acts as a protective layer for the flower's reproductive parts.

Petiole Leaf-stalk; some are adapted to give a climber support.

pH Scale from 0 to 14 that defines the alkalinity or acidity of soil. A pH of 7.0 is neutral; figures above this indicate increasing alkalinity, and those below increasing acidity. The acidity of soil can be assessed by using either a pH soil-testing kit, or by inserting a probe into the soil and reading the pH value on a dial (this is ideal for gardeners who are red/green colour blind). Most plants grow in a pH of 6.5–7.0.

Physic(k) garden Garden or specific area primarily devoted to growing medicinal plants.

Pillar rose Both rambling and climbing roses can be used to clothe pillars, which are usually rustic poles about 2.1 m (7 ft) high and often cut from conifers.

Plantlets Small, immature plants that develop on some leaves or at the ends of stems.

Pollarding Cutting a tree's branches hard back to near the trunk. It is usually performed because there is insufficient space for the branches to develop fully.

Pollination Alighting of pollen (male part) on the stigma (female part) of a flower. Fertilization does not necessarily follow pollination.

Posy (pl. posies) Small bunch of flowers, usually fragrant. A more recent term for nosegay.

Pricking off Initial moving of seedlings from where they were sown in pots or seed-trays (flats) to wider spacings in other seed-trays or pots.

Propagation Increasing your stock of plants by creating new ones by various methods from seeds to cuttings.

Propagator Enclosed plastic- or glass-covered unit in which seeds are encouraged to germinate and cuttings to root. Some propagators are heated.

Pruning Controlled removal of stems and shoots to encourage a plant to form a better shape, develop fruits and flowers and, in a few instances, produce attractive stems. It is also performed to remove congested and dead wood, allowing air to circulate more freely throughout the plant.

Pyramidal Having the shape of a pyramid and often used to describe the shapes of trees and conifers. Some topiary figures have a formal and pyramid shape, and some fruit trees are grown as pyramids.

Rambling roses (ramblers) These bear many large bunches of small flowers. Unfortunately, flowering is usually just for a single period in summer each year.

Reconstituted stone Used to construct a wide range of plant containers and ornaments. It mellows to a pleasing colour. Unfortunately, it does not have much constructional strength and therefore should not be knocked or put under pressure.

Re-used growing-bags Growing-bags that have been used for one season can be re-used during the following one. However, they first need topping up with peat and fertilizers.

Rhizomes Horizontal, creeping, underground or partly underground stems which act as a storage organ. Can be divided and encouraged to produce further plants.

Root cuttings Method of increasing certain plants by cutting up roots and inserting them either vertically or horizontally in well-aerated compost in pots or seed-trays (flats).

Seed-tray (flat) Flat-based tray in which seeds are sown and seedlings grown.

Semi-hardwood cuttings Another term for half-ripe cuttings.

Semi-mature cuttings Another term for half-ripe cuttings.

Shrubs Woody plants with several stems growing from ground level. Some plants can be grown as a tree or shrub, depending on the initial training and pruning.

Sink gardens Unusual and distinctive way to grow small plants, such as miniature conifers, alpine plants and miniature bulbs. Stone sinks are best, but glazed types can be modified, as well as new ones constructed from a mixture of cement powder, sharp sand and finely granulated peat.

Species Botanical classification within a genus. There may be one or several species within a genus.

Specimen plant Plant that is grown on its own to create a special display or feature.

Sphagnum moss Type of moss, earlier and widely used to line wire-framed hanging-baskets to assist in moisture retention and to prevent compost spilling out of the container. It also creates an attractive feature on the surfaces of hanging-baskets.

Spit Depth of the blade of a garden spade, 25–30 cm (10–12 in).

Spring-flowering bedding plants Medleys of biennial plants and spring-flowering bulbs, especially tulips, that are planted in beds and borders in late summer and early autumn, for flowering in spring and early summer of the following year.

Standard Plant grown on a single stem, with a long and bare area between the ground and the lowest branches. Many fruit trees and roses, as well as ornamental trees, are grown as standards.

Stool Usually means the roots of cut-down chrysanthemums. Also refers to some shrubs with masses of shoots that grow from ground level.

Stooling Cutting down woody stems to just above soil level to encourage the development of fresh shoots. A few shrubs are treated this way annually in spring, including some willows and dogwoods.

Strain Seed-raised plants from a common ancestor.

Subsoil Soil below the normal depth at which the soil is cultivated. Often, it has a heavy and clay-like texture.

Sucker Shoot that grows from a stem or root of a grafted or budded plant, and from below the position where the varietal part and the rootstock were united.

Summer-flowering bedding plants Frost-tender bedding plants (usually half-hardy annuals), raised in gentle warmth in late winter and early spring and planted into beds and borders in early summer, when all risk of frost has passed.

Synonym Alternative name for a plant (usually a superseded one).

Terrace Open, paved area immediately outside a house. Sometimes they are on several levels which are united by flights of steps.

Terracotta (also terra-cotta) Hardy, brownish-red material formed of clay, fine sand and, occasionally, pulverized pottery waste. This is made into containers, usually unglazed, for plants.

Thinning Removing congested seedlings to leave healthy ones with more space in which to develop and grow strongly.

Tip cuttings Softwood cuttings formed from a growing tip, piece of stem and a few leaves.

Topsoil Top layer of soil in which most plants grow.

Transplanting Moving young plants from a nursery bed to the positions in which they will grow and mature. This term is also used when large and established plants are moved.

Trees Woody-stemmed plants with a clear stem (trunk) between the roots and the lowest branches.

Tree-tie Method of securing a trunk to a support. Some are plastic; in earlier times, thick coir string was used. The tie must be adjustable to allow for expansion of the trunk.

Trunk Main stem of a tree.

Tuber Thickened, fleshy root (dahlia) or an underground stem (potato). These can be increased by division.

Urn Vase of varying shape and ornamentation made of glass-fibre, metal, plastic or reconstituted stone. Because of the limited amount of compost they can hold, they are mainly used for summer-flowering plants.

Variegated Mainly applied to leaves, and used to describe a state of having two or more colours.

Variety Naturally occurring variation within a plant. At one time, all variations within a species were known as varieties. Now, correctly, varieties raised in cultivation are known as cultivars.

Vegetative Refers to propagation and includes methods of increasing plants, such as by cuttings, layers, grafting, budding and division (but not seeds, which are part of the sexual reproduction process).

Verandah (also veranda) Term originating in India, describing a gallery at ground level and on one side of a house (occasionally, completely surrounding it). The roof is sloped to shed water and the sides partly or wholly open on the garden side.

Vermiculite Moisture-retentive material added to compost.

Versailles planter Large, square-sided container which originated at Versailles, France. Early ones were made of lead or slate, while modern types are usually constructed of wood or glass-fibre.

Vertical stake Method of supporting a tree by inserting a stake vertically into the ground before it is planted. If inserted afterwards, the roots of the tree may be damaged. The top of the stake should be fractionally below the lowest branch.

Wall shrubs Shrubs that can be grown and trained against a wall. Some wall shrubs are hardy and withstand low temperatures; others are tender and require the comfort of a warm and sunny wall.

Weeping Having a cascading habit, used to describe the outline of a tree or conifer. Some roses are grown as weeping standards and half-standards.

Whip and tongue grafting Method of propagation used to create some fruit trees.

Index

Photographs: Garden Matters (pages 7B, 8B, 9C AND BR, 66 and 68), King's Seeds (page 6BL AND BR),
Peter McHoy (pages 4BL and 9BL AND TR), Spear & Jackson (pages 14-15 and 18-20),
David Squire (pages 4EXCEPT BL, 8T, 46, 48 and 56) and Stephen Evans of Golden Days Garden Centre (page 60).
Other photographs by AG&G Books.